Desks

DESKS

Outstanding Projects from America's Best Craftsmen

WITH PLANS AND COMPLETE INSTRUCTIONS
FOR BUILDING 7 CLASSIC DESKS

ANDY CHARRON

The Taunton Press

Publisher: Jim Childs
Associate publisher: Helen Albert
Associate editor: Strother Purdy
Editor: Paul Anthony
Copy editor: Candace B. Levy
Indexer: Lynda Stannard
Cover designer: Steve Hughes
Interior designer: Lori Wendin
Layout artist: Suzie Yannes
Front cover photographer: Rob Karosis
Back cover photographer: Robert North
Interior photographer: Robert North
Illustrator: Melanie Powell

Taunton
BOOKS & VIDEOS
for fellow enthusiasts

Text ©2000 by Andy Charron
Photographs ©2000 by The Taunton Press, Inc.
Illustrations ©2000 by The Taunton Press, Inc.

Printed in the United States of America
10 9 8 7 6 5 4 3 2 1

The Taunton Press, Inc.,
63 South Main Street, PO Box 5506, Newtown, CT 06470-5506

e-mail: tp@taunton.com

Distributed by Publishers Group West

Library of Congress Cataloging-in-Publication Data
Charron, Andy.
     Desks : outstanding projects from America's best craftsmen : with plans and
complete instructions for building 7 classic desks / Andy Charron.
          p.   cm. — (Step-by-step)
     ISBN 1-56158-348-0
       1. Desks. 2. Furniture making. I. Title.
TT197.5.D4C48   2000
684.1'4—dc21   00-041157

ABOUT YOUR SAFETY

Working with wood is inherently dangerous. Using hand or power tools improperly or ignoring standard safety practices can lead to permanent injury or even death. Don't try to perform operations you learn about here (or elsewhere) unless you're certain they are safe for you. If something about an operation doesn't feel right, don't do it. Look for another way. We want you to enjoy the craft, so please keep safety foremost in your mind whenever you're working with wood.

For Brian

ACKNOWLEDGMENTS

This book never would have happened without the help and generosity of a number of people. In particular, I am especially indebted to all of the talented woodworkers who originally designed and built the desks presented here. I would like to thank Michael Wilson, Paul Wilson, Jim Becker, Stephen Lauziere, Thomas Stangeland, and Terry Moore. I am grateful for their infinite patience and cheerful willingness to drop what they were doing to answer my endless questions. The knowledge and little tricks they shared with me not only made this a better book but helped me attain a finer appreciation for these truly skilled craftsmen.

I would also like to thank the New Hampshire Furnituremasters Association and the New Hampshire Historical Society for allowing me to invade their gallery for a day to photograph one of the desks in their exhibit. The same goes for George Kachikis and E. Dale Collins who graciously opened their home to me, a total stranger, and allowed me to rearrange half the furniture in their house so I could get a few photos of their desk.

Finally, I would like to express my appreciation to all the people who worked behind the scenes to help create this book. In particular, I would like to thank Robert North and Jerry LeBlond who took most of the photos found on these pages. Their attention to detail, patience, and ability to see things I would miss continually amazed me. Thanks also go to the people at The Taunton Press, including Helen Albert, and especially Strother Purdy. I would also like to add a special note of thanks to Paul Anthony. It may be my name on the cover, but it was Paul's editorial skills that truly shaped this book.

Contents

INTRODUCTION

Desks have always occupied a unique spot in the world of furniture. They can be massive, intimidating seats of power behind which monumental decisions are made, or they may be simple utilitarian stands on which mundane tasks like paying bills are preformed. In fact, the design and construction of a desk often reflects the personality of its owner. Most woodworkers, me included, dream of someday building the ultimate desk. Functional yet beautiful, strong yet graceful, this ideal desk not only challenges our woodworking skills but serves as a lasting testimony to the character of its creator.

A typical desk must combine the structural elements of a table, the strength of bookshelves and the engineering of an entertainment center. A well-built desk may also have more drawers than a large dresser and will often require the knowledge of several different types of joinery. As a result, designing and building a desk can be a somewhat intimidating task. However, if each element is viewed as a separate component, combining them to create a beautiful and functional desk is no more difficult than building any other piece of furniture.

The purpose of this book is to provide a step-by-step guide to anyone who aspires to build his or her dream desk. It is divided into two main sections. The first chapter discusses the general concepts of desk design and construction. A typical desk is broken down into components that are described in detail. Particular attention is given to sizing components, material selection, and appropriate hardware. Joinery, specialty applications like hidden drawers, and finishing techniques are also discussed.

The bulk of the book is devoted to seven specific desks, covering a broad range of styles and degrees of difficulty. Each chapter features detailed measured drawings and sequence photos of some of the more interesting or challenging aspects of construction. In addition, each chapter focuses on a particular aspect of woodworking. For example, one chapter provides information about cutting dovetail joints, whereas another may provide a step-by-step guide to working with figured veneers. When taken as a whole, the detailed sections in each chapter should combine to form a complete reference of techniques that can be used to create any project imaginable.

You will notice that each chapter is broken down into a series of steps that follow a logical sequence. However, there may be occasions when you want to jump ahead to another aspect of the project before returning to complete the parts you skipped. Or you may want to incorporate an element from one desk into a design found in another chapter. I would recommend that you read through the entire chapter first before beginning a project. I think if you begin by understanding *how* a piece was put together, you will have a better sense of *why* certain tasks are best performed in the prescribed order.

Although I have tried to be faithful to the original design and construction process used to create each of the desks presented here, certainly nothing is set in stone. You may use a different method of cutting a particular joint or you may alter the dimensions, design, or materials used to create a particular desk. Or you may copy a desk exactly as it was originally built. However you choose to proceed, think of this book as a guide that will help you create your own personalized desk that is both beautiful and functional.

Desk-Building Basics

DESIGNING AND BUILDING a desk can be a very satisfying project. A well-built, well-designed desk can provide a home or office with both utility and beauty. It's hard to imagine a piece of furniture that gets more intimate use than a desk. We use it to write letters, do finances, and schedule our week.

Designing a desk can be challenging, particularly if it needs to satisfy a variety of needs. But just remember that a desk—like any other piece of furniture—is nothing more than a collection of different components that fit together. All desks consist of two basic elements: a top that serves as a writing surface and a base that supports it. When each component is considered separately, a desk really is no more complicated than a set of bookshelves, a table, or a chest of drawers.

When designing a desk, keep in mind the old tried-and-true design maxim: Form follows function. Ask yourself how the desk will be used, and where. Will it serve as an office workstation or will it be used strictly for writing an occasional letter? Does it have to be sized to fit in a certain area, and does it need to match existing furniture? Is it going to do double-duty as a bookcase or a side table? Think it through as carefully as you can, and you're bound to produce a piece of useful, lovely furniture that will serve you for years.

PARTS OF A DESK

Base

Even the most basic desk in this book—the Lap Desk (p. 20)—must have a writing surface that is supported by a base. The base may be as simple as a box, as fundamental as four legs joined by an apron, or as complex as a pair of drawer pedestals joined by a paneled back. Ultimately, the base determines the type of desk and should combine functionality with aesthetics and strength. A base that's too small or poorly constructed may result in a writing surface that shakes and wiggles. On the other hand, a massive base may appear out of proportion to its top.

Writing surface

The main thing to consider when designing the top of a desk is how it will be used and what will be placed on it. A desk used solely for writing letters doesn't need a very large top, whereas an office desk that will hold a computer, books, and papers will require a relatively large working surface.

The construction of the writing surface can be as simple as a glued-up board or it can be as complex as you like, adding shaping or detailing with moldings or veneers. In any case, the top is usually the most visible part of a desk, so pay careful attention to the boards you choose for it. In addition, you can aug-

Same Case, Different Bases

ATTACHING THE SAME DESK CASE to different bases greatly alters the look of the entire piece.

CONTEMPORARY FALL-FRONT DESK

CHIPPENDALE-STYLE FALL-FRONT DESK
ON A CHEST OF DRAWERS

QUEEN ANNE–STYLE FALL-FRONT DESK

ment the top with leather or glass. A leather overlay provides a writing surface that is firm, yet soft and comfortable. A glass top not only provides a smooth, hard surface on which to work, it also protects the wood underneath.

Drawers, pigeonholes, and shelves

A simple writing table may need only one or two shallow drawers to hold pens, pencils, and papers; but some small desks are also outfitted with compartments for holding letters, bills, stamps, and writing supplies (see the photo at right). Larger desks, made for home or professional office use, usually incorporate a number of larger drawers, including at least one file-size drawer. A computer workstation may require a pull-out tray for a keyboard as well as a large compartment for the computer case and perhaps a pull-out shelf for a printer or other computer peripheral.

Desks designed for holding letters, bills, and stamps sometimes incorporate a number of small compartments in the case.

Open shelving on a desk can accommodate everything from computer components to plants and books.

Shelves can be added to a desk to press it into double-duty as bookcase. The easiest approach is simply to install open shelving above the desktop (see the bottom photo on the facing page). A large, complex desk such as a traditional secretary often conceals a series of shelves behind doors above the writing surface (see the photo at right). Another alternative is to house shelves in a separate cabinet placed on top of the desk.

SIZING THE COMPONENTS

Working at a desk that is either too small or too large can be extremely frustrating. An undersize desk promotes overstuffed drawers and high piles of unorganized clutter on the desktop. On the other hand, an oversize desk can unnecessarily take up a lot of room and put your papers out of reach. Here are a few considerations to help you determine the proper size for a desk.

Working surface

The size of the top ultimately determines the overall size of the desk, so it's wise to consider it first. When determining how big to make the top, you must consider not only how it will be used but what may be placed on it. If your desk will be used for simple tasks like writing letters or paying bills, you won't need a very large top. For example, the working surface of the Lap Desk (p. 20) is less than 2 ft. square. On the other hand, a desk designed for a busy home or professional office must have a much larger working area, such as that of the 12-ft.-square top on the Pedestal Desk (p. 124).

Obviously, if you plan on placing a shelving unit, a computer, a printer, and a fax machine on top of a desk, the working surface must be considerable. If you decide to go the route of a large computer workstation, you may want to incorporate several different working areas into your desk, including

A traditional secretary combines the elements of a desk and a bookcase by blending the two units into one piece.

additional extensions to create an L- or U-shaped unit.

Leg room

When sizing a desk, make sure to build in enough height and width for leg room in the knee well. The height of the knee well is based on the height of the working surface. Typical desk height is between 29 in. and 30 in., which makes for comfortable writing, reading, or talking on the phone when seated in a normal chair, which is about 18 in. high. The ideal height for a computer keyboard, however, is lower, at about 26 in. (see "Ideal Desk Dimensions" on p. 8). This presents a design challenge: If you make the top of the desk low enough for comfortable keyboard use, then a center drawer or supporting skirt is out of the question, because it would hit

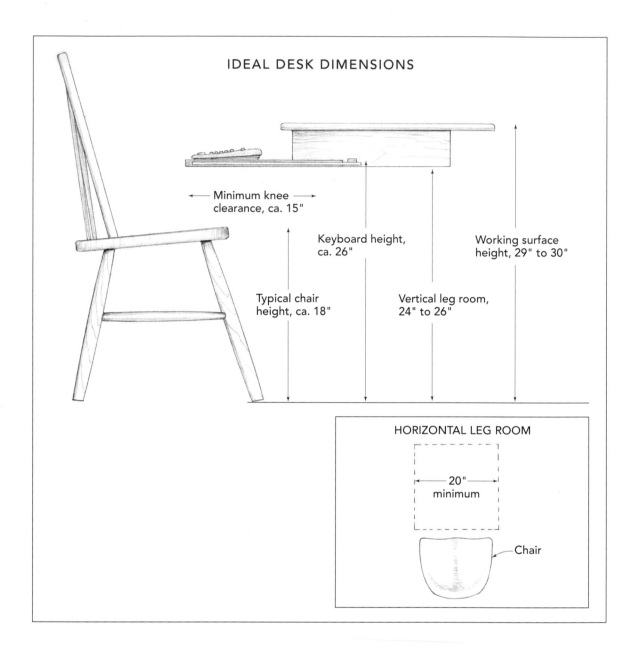

IDEAL DESK DIMENSIONS

Minimum knee clearance, ca. 15"

Keyboard height, ca. 26"

Working surface height, 29" to 30"

Typical chair height, ca. 18"

Vertical leg room, 24" to 26"

HORIZONTAL LEG ROOM

20" minimum

Chair

your knees. One solution is to place the keyboard on a pull-out tray mounted under a 30-in.-high desktop, like the Laptop Desk (p. 54). However you design your desk, the vertical leg room should be an absolute minimum of 24 in. high, although 26 in. is ideal.

As for the width of the knee well, it can be as small as 20 in. wide, as long as the desk is simply used for writing and the chair is relatively immobile. However, if you wheel your chair around a lot to access a computer on one end of the desk and a phone and fax machine on the other, you'll need more leg room. In this case, allow an opening of at least 24 in. wide.

Storage needs

To determine the necessary size and number of desk drawers, shelves, and compartments, first assess what they will hold. They may be sized to accommodate envelopes, pens, paper, books, computer disks and peripherals, CDs, and files. If you anticipate putting certain objects in particular compartments, size them accordingly (see "Pigeonhole Inserts"). Make your shelves and compartments deep enough

PIGEONHOLE INSERTS

The size, number, and position of doors, drawers, and shelves determine the look
and function of a pigeonhole insert.

to hold the largest objects you intend to place on them, and make them sturdy enough to prevent sagging over time.

When designing file drawers, there are two major considerations: the size of the files and whether they will fit in the drawer from front to back or from side to side. Letter-size file folders are about 11¾ in. by 9½ in., whereas legal-size file folders are 14¾ in. by 9½ in. (see "File Drawer Dimensions"). Also consider whether the file folders will simply stand in the drawer or whether they will be placed in the type of dividers that hang from wooden or metal tracks fastened to the drawer. If you want to use hanging dividers, you must add at least 1¼ in. to the width of the drawer. If you plan to use a commercially made, freestanding hanging file rack in the drawer, check its size before designing the drawer.

MATERIALS

The materials and hardware that you select make a big difference in the overall quality of the desk. A good design can be ruined by the use of inappropriate materials. Most of the desks in this book use a combination of materials. The visible parts are generally made of a combination of solid wood and plywood. The interior components are usually made of a lesser grade of hardwood, and the drawers are often made of a softwood, like pine.

Solid wood, plywood, and medium-density fiberboard

Although you could argue that the use of solid hardwood is the true mark of fine furniture, it doesn't mean that composite materials like plywood or medium-density fiberboard (MDF) can't be used in a top-quality desk.

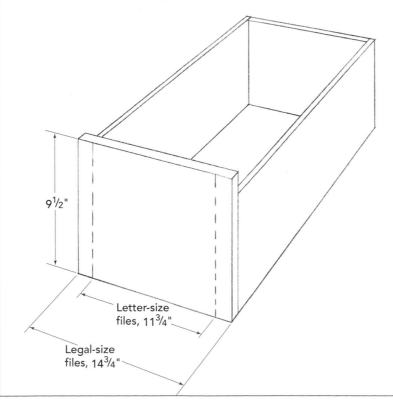

FILE DRAWER DIMENSIONS

To accommodate standard file folders, a file drawer must have a minimum depth of 9½" and a width of either 11¾" for letter-size files or 14¾" for legal-size files. If the drawer will include a commercially made rack for hanging dividers, check the size of the hardware before building the drawer.

9½"

Letter-size files, 11³/₄"

Legal-size files, 14³/₄"

Plywood is an ideal material for large surfaces like cabinet sides, backs, tops, and shelves. Solid-wood moldings and details dress up the edges of the plywood.

Many finely crafted pieces of modern furniture, like this writing table, are made primarily of MDF covered with highly figured veneers.

In fact, plywood is an excellent choice for large surfaces that must remain relatively flat and stable. It is less expensive than quality hardwood, won't crack, and is much less prone to warpage. I generally use plywood for large parts, like case sides and shelves, or for parts that won't be readily seen, like drawer bottoms and cabinet backs. I have also used cabinet-grade plywood with good-quality veneered faces for flat door panels and desktops (see the photo on the facing page).

MDF is a dense, high-quality form of particleboard that is smooth, flat, and very stable. It is an excellent substrate on which to glue expensive veneer. Actually, a surprising amount of the finest hand-crafted furniture made today is built of veneered MDF (see the photo above). Standard particleboard—which is often used in commercially produced, economy office furniture—is a poor choice for a desk that you plan to use for years. Be aware that particleboard doesn't hold screws as well as hardwood or plywood. Under heavy use, it can crumble and eventually fall apart (see the photo at right).

Particleboard, often used in low-grade commercial furniture, doesn't hold fasteners well, particularly in end-grain applications like this drawer joint.

HARDWARE

The hardware used to build some desks, like the Greene and Greene Writing Desk (p. 70), may be limited to a few screws. Other projects incorporate drawer slides, hinges, and locks. How well a desk functions depends a great deal on the quality of the hardware used. Although the most expensive hardware is not necessarily the best, I recommend using the best quality available. It doesn't make sense to spend hundreds of dollars on wood, devote numerous hours to building a project, and then try to save a few bucks on a set of cheap drawer slides or hinges that will eventually break, jam, or sag.

Drawer slides

Without a doubt, the least expensive drawer slides are made of wood; however, they are not always the appropriate solution. For example, if desk drawers are going to suffer heavy use in a busy office, it makes sense to use smooth-rolling, heavy-duty metal slides. Good-quality, commercially produced drawer slides are relatively inexpensive and easy to install. They virtually guarantee that a drawer will open and close easily for years (see the left photo below).

Locks

Depending on what you store in your desk, you may want to lock one or all of the drawers or doors. Cylinder locks are an inexpensive way to lock drawers, whereas full-mortise locks are a more secure way to lock cabinet drawers and doors (see the right photo below). If you build a desk with a bank of drawers, you may want to incorporate a

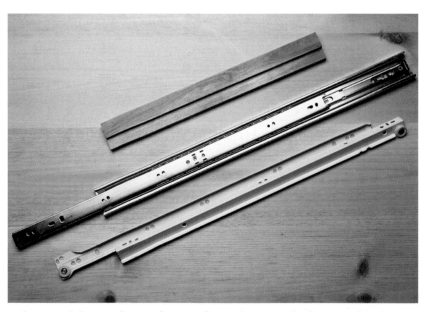

A drawer slide may be made out of wood or metal. The unpainted metal slide shown here mounts at any height on the side of a drawer. The white one mounts on the bottom edge of the drawer side.

The cylinder lock on the left is a relatively inexpensive option for locking drawers. The full-mortise lock on the right is more secure and suited to both drawers and doors.

system designed for locking two or more drawers at a time.

CONSTRUCTION TECHNIQUES

Basic joinery

For a quick review of some of the basic joints you'll find in this book, see the photos at right and on p. 14.

Building secret compartments

Secret drawers and compartments add a unique touch to any desk. Although none of the desks in this book contains secret compartments, they could easily be added by making slight alterations to the basic design. For example, you can readily create a hiding place by adding a false bottom to a drawer. Another approach is to tuck a small box behind a shortened drawer. Attaching a loose divider to the box makes it easy to pull out (see "Secret Compartments" on p. 15). Whatever sort of compartment you make, the trick to concealing it is to make the joinery tight and precise. And hide any seams by placing them adjacent to normal joint lines.

Dealing with wood movement

Wood is an inherently unstable material. It expands and contracts with seasonal changes in humidity and temperature. It's important to take this into account when designing and building furniture. Failure to accommodate wood movement can result in joints that break apart; moldings that fall off; and panels that warp, crack, or even split wide open (see the photo on p. 16).

The main things to remember are that wood expands and contracts primarily across the grain and that the wider the board, the more it will move. Movement along the grain, however, is negligible. That is, boards don't typically become much shorter or longer. So the challenge is really how to join pieces

A dado joint is a butt joint enclosed in a three-sided channel, called a dado. The larger glue area and the shoulders of the joint combine to make this much stronger than a simple butt joint.

A rabbet joint is a butt joint that is restrained on one side by a ledge, called a rabbet, that is cut into the mating piece. The joint is not as strong as a dado joint and is often reinforced with screws, nails, or other mechanical fasteners.

Dovetail joints are attractive and extremely strong, although somewhat challenging to make. The large glue surface and locking tails and pins make this a great joint for solid-wood drawer and case corners.

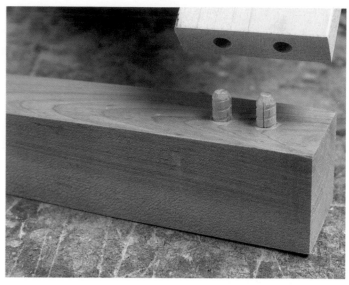

Dowel joinery is used extensively in commercial applications. If you have the right equipment, accurate joints are quick to produce, although they are only moderately strong.

Mortise-and-tenon joints are ideal for joining solid wood at a right angle, even if the pieces are of different sizes and shapes. They are frequently used for joining table skirts to legs.

Biscuit joinery is an attractive small-shop alternative to dowels or stub tenons. The joints, which are easily cut with a biscuit joiner or router, are quick to assemble and allow for some lateral adjustment of the joint during assembly.

Secret Compartments

FALSE-BOTTOM DRAWER

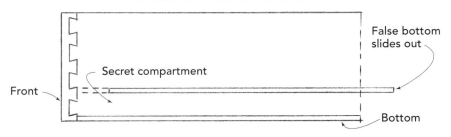

False bottom slides out

Secret compartment

Front

Bottom

To create a hidden space within a drawer, install a secondary, false bottom.

DRAWER BEHIND A DRAWER

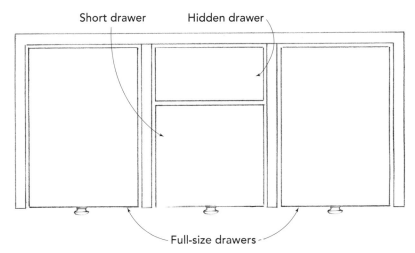

OVERHEAD VIEW OF HIDDEN DRAWER

Short drawer

Hidden drawer

Full-size drawers

A small box tucked behind a shortened drawer provides a convenient hiding place.

HIDDEN COMPARTMENT WITH A HANDLE

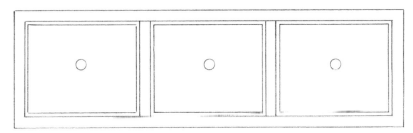

FRONT VIEW, DRAWERS WITH DIVIDERS

A loose divider attached to a hidden compartment becomes a handle.

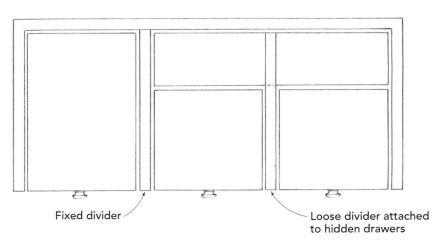

OVERHEAD VIEW

Fixed divider

Loose divider attached to hidden drawers

cross-grain to each other. The easiest solution is to avoid cross-grain problems in the first place by orienting the grain of all the boards in the same direction (see "Designing for Wood Movement"). This is particularly applicable to solid-wood case construction.

One common approach to preventing wood movement problems in large panels is to use frame-and-panel joinery, which allows a panel to expand and contract freely within the grooves of a frame (see "Designing for Wood Movement"). When sizing floating panels to fit their frames, you need to take into account the local climate and season of year as well as the type of wood you're using. If you live in a relatively dry, unchanging climate you can make the panels fairly tight. If you live in an area that undergoes significant seasonal changes, you have to allow for more movement. Also, the time of year must be taken

Wood expands and contracts across the grain only. The molding on this case was glued cross-grain to the dovetailed case side, creating a crack as the case side shrank.

DESIGNING FOR WOOD MOVEMENT

SOLID-WOOD CASE JOINERY

When joining solid-wood case pieces, orient the grain in the same direction on all of the boards so they expand and contract harmoniously.

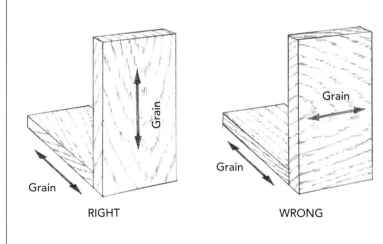

RIGHT   WRONG

FRAME-AND-PANEL CONSTRUCTION

In a frame-and-panel assembly, the panel floats unglued in frame grooves, allowing it to expand and contract with seasonal changes.

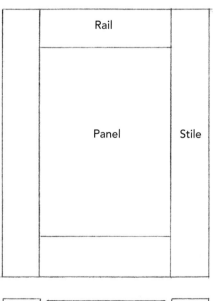

Rail

Panel   Stile

Stile   END VIEW

into account. If you are building your project in the winter, when the air is dry, you should leave more room for expansion than if you are building in the summer, when it's humid.

The type of wood also factors into your wood movement calculations. Red oak, for example, can expand and contract as much as ¼ in. over 1 ft., whereas teak may move only ⅛ in. over the same width. For many woods, you can count on movement somewhere within that range. A final word: Never glue a solid-wood panel into a frame. The glue will lock the panel in place, eventually causing it to crack or split.

FINISHING TECHNIQUES

Most furniture makers I know have strong opinions on the subject of finishing. Either they find it an enjoyable final step in a project well done or they consider it a necessary evil, attacking it with a certain sense of fear and dread. Regardless of where you stand on the issue, you'll want to put a good-quality protective finish on your completed desk. For each desk in this book I briefly describe the finish that was originally used and how it was applied. The descriptions are intended as only a guide. You may find that the finish and method of application are beyond your present capabilities or you may just want to try something different.

Finishing is a complex process involving many different materials and a variety of tools and application techniques. When choosing your finish, there are a few factors to consider. First, determine the appropriate finish for a particular desk based on its use. For example, if it will be primarily a showpiece, a hand-rubbed oil-and-wax finish may be appropriate. However, if it's going to serve duty in a commercial office, a much more durable finish, such as a urethane or catalyzed lacquer, would be a better selection.

Your choices depend somewhat on your finishing facilities. If you have spray equipment and a finishing booth with explosion-proof lights and ventilation fans, your finishing

options are almost unlimited. On the other hand, if you do your finishing in a basement with poor ventilation, you're pretty much limited to wiping or brushing on finishes like oil, shellac, and polyurethane. In any case, the best advice I can offer is that if you are trying something that you've never used before, first experiment on scrap wood before tackling your project.

Applying an oil finish

Until I bought my first spray gun, the only finish I used was hand-rubbed oil. Oil finishes look great, go on easily, and offer more than enough protection for most projects. You don't need any special equipment, and dust is never a problem.

Although there are many methods for applying an oil finish, I try to keep the process as simple as possible. I begin by sanding the wood with 220-grit sandpaper. Then I use a clean cloth to flood the surface with a heavy coat of oil. After a few minutes I use another clean cloth to wipe off as much of the oil as possible. After an hour or so, I wipe it down again with a clean, dry cloth before letting it dry for the night. (*Note: Oil-soaked rags are highly flammable and must be either immersed in water or laid out flat to dry before being thrown away.*)

Depending on the type of wood, the quality of the finish I want, and how much time I have, I may apply only two coats of oil or I may put on as many as seven. If the surface seems rough, I may sand between coats, using progressively finer grits. I usually stop at 320 grit. I may even use steel wool to apply the oil. Finally, if I want the finish to have a soft luster, I let it cure for a week or two before buffing on a coat of furniture wax.

There are many types of oil finishes available, and they have different cure times. If a finish is labeled as "pure" tung or linseed oil, it can take weeks to dry. Most commercially available wiping oils, however, include metallic dryers to greatly speed up the curing process. If you're unsure of the finish, test the drying time on scrap wood.

Drawer Corner Joinery Options

THE JOINTS USED FOR DRAWER CONSTRUCTION can create a subtle design touch or make a big splash if you expose the end grain through dovetails. The joints can be the most time-consuming aspect of a desk project, or they can fly by in an hour or two if you use machine-cut rabbets. They can be easy to assemble and require little clamping, or they can be a bear and put a dent in your clamp rack.

Through dovetails: Aesthetically pleasing and very strong, the through dovetail can be used on either the front or the back or both.

Half-blind dovetails: Traditionally used for drawer fronts, this joint provides the strength of a dovetail with a more formal look.

Rabbeted half dovetail: This machine-cut joint requires one pass on the router table for each component. It can be pinned with dowels for additional strength.

Sliding dovetails: A very strong alternative that locks the sides into the front. This joint requires a very precise fit and can be difficult to assemble.

Blind dado rabbet: This is a production joint that can be cut quickly on the table saw or a router table. It looks good when the parts fit precisely.

LAP DESK

If the briefcase was the precursor to today's laptop computers, then lap desks were the forerunners of briefcases. Like a briefcase, a lap desk is good for carrying important papers and writing implements. Lap desks were commonly used in the eighteenth and nineteenth centuries by people whose work required a lot of traveling.

In today's world, with palm-size portable computers, there may not seem much need for a lap desk. But it does have a place in the modern home as a phone message center. Your local phone book should fit neatly in the drawer, and there is plenty of room inside the compartment for note pads, pens, and pencils. This desk would also make an ideal "first desk" for a small child.

This particular desk is a variation of a common Shaker design. The box walls and top are made of solid cherry, whereas the shelf and bottom are made of hardwood plywood to prevent wood movement problems. Although it is the smallest and easiest project in this book, this desk does call for two different types of dovetail joints. The box sides are joined with through dovetails, and the drawer front is attached to the sides with half-blind dovetails. Although you could use a router and a dovetail jig to make the joints, I prefer to cut them by hand on a project this small.

Lap Desk

THE DESK IS BASICALLY A DOVETAILED BOX with a shelf and drawer inside. The two-piece top consists of a rail and a hinged lid. The two pieces are capped with breadboard ends to restrict warpage. The plywood shelf sits in stopped grooves in the box sides, and the plywood bottom is edged with molding and screwed to the box bottom.

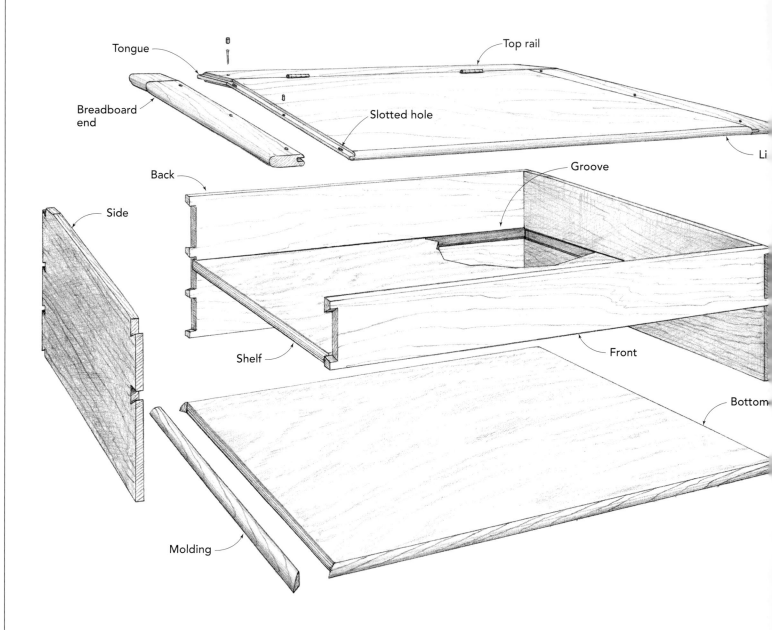

Tongue

Top rail

Breadboard end

Slotted hole

Li

Back

Groove

Side

Shelf

Front

Bottom

Molding

FRONT VIEW

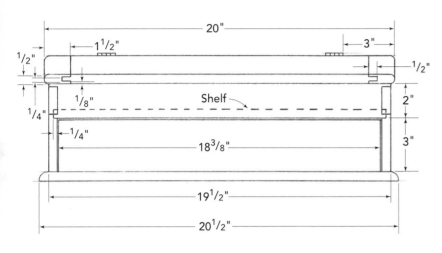

SIDE VIEW

Drawer removed

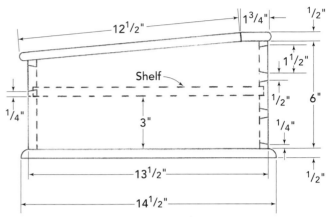

DRAWER

Bottom overhang
serves as drawer stop.

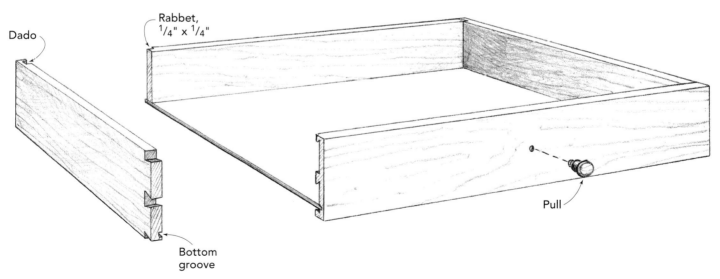

Dado

Rabbet,
1/4" x 1/4"

Bottom
groove

Pull

BUILDING THE DESK STEP-BY-STEP

CUT LIST FOR LAP DESK

Case

2	Sides	½ in. x 6 in. x 13½ in.
1	Front	½ in. x 2 in. x 19½ in.
1	Back	½ in. x 6 in. x 19½ in.
1	Bottom	½ in. x 13½ in. x 19½ in., hardwood plywood
1	Shelf	½ in. x 13 in. x 19 in., hardwood plywood
1	Top	½ in. x 1¾ in. x 18 in. (including a ¼-in. x ½-in. tongue on both ends)
2	Top breadboard ends	½ in. x 1½ in. x 1¾ in.
1	Lid	½ in. x 12½ in. x 18 in. (including a ¼-in. x ½-in. tongue on both ends)
2	Lid breadboard ends	½ in. x 1½ in. x 12½ in.

Drawer

1	Drawer front	½ in. x 3 in. x 18⅜ in.
2	Drawer sides	½ in. x 3 in. x 12⅝ in.
1	Drawer back	½ in. x 2¾ in. x 17⅞ in.
1	Drawer bottom	⅛ in. x 12¾ in. x 17⅜ in., plywood
1	Drawer knob	

Miscellaneous

¼-in. diameter	Walnut dowel	
1 pair	Butt hinge	1 in. x 1 in. (open)
6 lineal ft.	Quarter-round molding	½ in. x ½ in.

THE DESK IS BASICALLY a dovetailed box with a hinged lid and a shelf and drawer inside. I make the box walls first, then assemble them with the shelf in between. After I attach the bottom, I make the top, attach it, then make and fit the drawer.

PREPARING THE STOCK

1. Thickness plane enough boards for the top, sides, front, and back of the desk.
2. Select your best-looking stock for the two-piece top. Although the top could be made from a single board, I think it is better to glue it up from two or three narrower boards to minimize warpage. If you have a highly figured piece of thick cherry, you may want to resaw and book-match stock for the top. (For more on resawing and book-matching, see Pedestal Desk, p. 124.)

MAKING THE BOX

Cutting the parts

1. Cut the pieces for the sides, back, and front, ripping them to width and crosscutting them to length.
2. Cut the angled top on each of the sides. You could do this on a bandsaw or with a jigsaw, but I prefer to use a tapering jig on a table saw, because it's the easiest way to make two matching, straight cuts (see **photo A** on p. 26).

Cutting the dovetails

Dovetails are both strong and beautiful. They may look a bit complicated to cut, but with sharp tools and a little practice you should be able to cut all of the dovetails for this project in a few hours. The size and spacing of the tails are matters of personal preference, although the angle of the tails should be somewhere between 12 and 14 degrees.

1. Begin by laying out the tails on both ends of each side piece (see **photo B** on p. 27). You could start by laying out and cutting the pins

A SHOPMADE TAPERING JIG

A tapering jig holds a workpiece at an angle for making tapered cuts. Commercial models cost only about $20, but you can also easily make one yourself.

To make the jig, hinge together two straight boards at one end, then attach a stop block to the board that will support the workpiece. Cut a slot along the center of a strip of plywood and attach it with one screw to the top edge of the board that will ride against the table saw fence. Run a screw through the slot into the fence board, using a washer underneath the screw to provide more bearing surface.

To use the jig, first mark the taper on your workpiece, then place the jig against the table saw fence with the workpiece placed against the jig's fence and stop block. Loosen the screw in the slot, position the fence at the proper angle to cut the taper, then retighten the screw. As you cut, hold the workpiece against the jig, using push sticks, if necessary, to keep your hands away from the blade.

A SHOPMADE TAPERING JIG

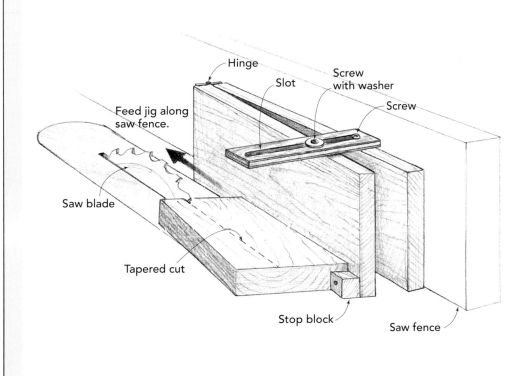

Hinge

Slot

Screw with washer

Screw

Feed jig along saw fence.

Saw blade

Tapered cut

Stop block

Saw fence

FIXING DOVETAIL MISTAKES

It's not uncommon to miscut dovetails. Here are a few approaches for fixing your mistakes.

If you remove too much waste from between the pins, fill the resulting gap by gluing a small shim to the tail, then shaping the shim before the joint is assembled.

You can fill a gap after assembly by gluing and tapping in a small wedge, then trimming it flush afterward (see photo at right).

On dark wood, small gaps can be filled with a mixture of epoxy and powdered graphite.

On lighter colored woods, you can use neutral colored wood filler or a mixture of sanding dust and glue.

Although it's difficult to make a mistake completely disappear, a carefully selected patch goes a long way toward hiding a miscut dovetail.

Photo A: A tapering jig allows you to cut straight, consistently accurate tapers, such as those needed on the box sides.

DOVETAIL JIGS

Cutting and fitting dovetails by hand can be very satisfying. However, if you have a lot of dovetails to make, cutting them by hand can quickly become a nightmare.

Dovetail jigs, which incorporate templates for guiding a router, are an alternative to hand-cut dovetails. These commercial jigs come in a variety of sizes and price ranges. In general, the more a jig can do, the more it costs. Less expensive models are designed to cut only one size and type of dovetail and offer only one spacing pattern. Although limited in function, these jigs can be ideal for drawer production. More expensive jigs can be used to create an infinite variety of through and half-blind dovetails.

In addition to the jig, you'll need to invest in a decent router and a few good-quality bits. If you cut dovetails only occasionally, it doesn't make sense to spend the money on a dovetail jig. However, if you plan on incorporating dovetails into your daily routine, you may want to check out these jigs.

Some dovetail jigs, like the one on the right, are designed to cut evenly spaced pins and tails; others, like the one on the left, can be adjusted to vary the spacing.

first, but I find it is easier to cut the tails first, and then use them as patterns for laying out the pins. I laid out three tails at the back and one in front (see "Side View" on p. 23).

2. Remove the waste from between each tail with a sharp saw. I use a bandsaw to cut close to the lines, then I finish paring to the lines with a sharp chisel (see **photo C** on p. 20).

3. Lay each set of tails on the end of their mating piece and trace their outlines to establish the cut lines for the pins. A thin line will yield a more accurate joint, so use a very sharp pencil or knife (see **photo D** on p. 28).

4. Use a saw and a chisel to clean out the waste between the pins. I waste away the bulk of the material with a bandsaw, then clean up the cut with a chisel (see **photo E** on p. 29). Check the fit of the joint frequently, removing tiny amounts of waste as you approach a perfect fit. The joint should be snug enough to require firm hand pressure to push it together,

Photo B: Use a bevel gauge and a sharp pencil to lay out the tails. To prevent mistakes, clearly mark the waste area to be removed.

Photo C: I rough cut the tails on a bandsaw. Afterward, I use a chisel to pare to the cut lines.

Photo D: I lay out the pins by tracing around the tails.

but it shouldn't be so tight that you need to beat it with a hammer.

Making the shelf and bottom

1. Rout the ¼-in.-deep by ½-in.-wide shelf grooves in the sides and back (see "Lap Desk" on p. 22). Stop the grooves ¼ in. shy of the ends of the pieces so they don't run through the ends of the tails or pins. Also rout the rabbet on the lower edge of the front piece. I routed the grooves on a router table, but a handheld router and a straightedge would work as well.

2. Dry-fit the box and measure for the plywood bottom and shelf.

3. Cut the bottom and the shelf, making sure they are perfectly square.

4. Dry-fit the box one more time to make sure the shelf fits properly.

Photo E: After notching the waste between the pins with a bandsaw, I chisel to the cut line.

Assembling the box

1. Disassemble the box and sand all of the parts, including the top face of the shelf.

2. Glue one side of the box to the back, slip the shelf into its grooves, then glue the front and remaining side in place (see **photo F**). As long as the plywood shelf fits properly, it doesn't need glue or fasteners to hold it in place.

3. After the glue has dried, fasten the bottom to the box with glue and several countersunk 1-in.-long screws. Make sure the bottom is cut square and that it lines up evenly around the bottom of the box. It's okay if the edges stick out a bit, because they can be sanded flush with the sides after the glue has dried.

4. Finish-sand all of the parts.

5. Make the quarter-round molding. I routed the ½-in.-radius roundover on a ½-in.-thick board, then ripped off the strip, repeating the process for each piece of molding. Although I

Photo F: If your dovetails fit properly, you should need to clamp the box in only one direction.

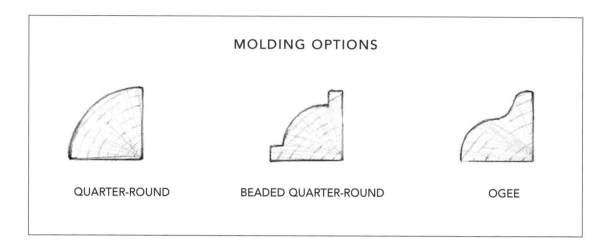

MOLDING OPTIONS

QUARTER-ROUND   BEADED QUARTER-ROUND   OGEE

chose to make quarter-round molding, you could use any profile bit you like (see "Molding Options").

6. Fit and attach the molding, mitering it at its corners. Glue and nail it into place on the edges of the bottom.

MAKING THE TOP

The top consists of a rail and a hinged lid, which are capped with breadboard ends to restrain warpage. The breadboard ends are attached with a tongue-and-groove joint that is glued only at its center. The ends of the joint are doweled through slotted holes, allowing the panel to expand and contract with seasonal changes.

Making the parts

1. Using your best-looking stock, glue up one panel big enough to make both the top rail and lid at once. Make the panel about ¼-in. oversize in length and width for now.

2. After the glue has dried, plane or sand the panel to ½ in. thick. Try to achieve a consistent thickness, because any variation will affect the thickness of the tongue and thus the fit of the breadboard end joint.

3. Crosscut the panel to length, being sure to include the length for the tongue on each end. Leave the panel oversize in width for now.

4. Make the stock for the two breadboard ends, leaving the pieces slightly oversize in length for now.

5. Using a dado head in the table saw, rip a ¼-in.-wide by ½-in.-deep groove in each of the breadboard ends, centering it in the edge of the stock.

6. Cut two opposing rabbets on each end of the panel to create the tongue (see "Lap Desk" on p. 22). I cut the rabbets using a dado head mounted in a table saw, but you could use a router instead. Make sure the tongues are centered on the ends of the panel and that they fit snugly into their grooves in the breadboard ends.

Attaching the breadboard ends

1. Dry-fit the breadboard ends onto the panel and mark for the dowel holes. The section that will be the rail gets one hole in each end. The section that will be the lid gets three holes on each end (see "Lap Desk" on p. 22).

2. Drill the holes, centering them across the length of the tongue.

3. Remove the breadboard ends and elongate the outermost holes about ⅛ in. on each side with a round file to allow the lid to expand and contract.

4. Cut eight ¾-in.-long pieces from a ¼-in.-diameter dowel.

Photo G: Notice
how the grain pat-
tern is continuous
between the lid and
top and the bread-
board ends.

5. Apply glue to the centermost few inches of
the tongue, then attach the breadboard ends
to the panel.

6. Tap the dowels into their holes, applying
just a bit of glue to the last ⅛ in. of each one
(see **photo G**).

7. After the glue dries, trim the dowels flush
and sand both faces of the panel assembly.

Fitting and attaching the top

1. Using a ¼-in.-radius roundover bit in a
router table, rout the bullnose profile on the
breadboard ends and the back edge of the
panel assembly. You'll cut the profile on the
front edge after ripping the lid to final width.

2. Rip the 1¾-in.-wide top rail from the panel
assembly, then cut a 5-degree bevel on its
inside edge (see "Side View" on p. 23). The
bevel allows the square edge of the lid to fit
snugly against the edge of the rail when the
lid is closed. You could cut the bevel on a
jointer, but I ripped it on the table saw (see
photo H).

Photo H: After sawing the rail from the top assembly, cut a 5-degree
bevel along its front edge.

3. Position the rail on the box, making sure that it overhangs evenly at the rear and that the bottom edge of the bevel lines up with the angles on the sides of the box.

4. Attach the rail. You could simply glue it to the box, but I decided to use three #6 by ¾-in. screws, countersinking them and capping them with walnut plugs.

5. Rip the lid to final width. To determine the width, measure from the front edge of the rail to a distance ½ in. out from the front of the box (see "Side View" on p. 23).

6. After ripping the lid, rout the bullnose on its front edge.

7. Mortise for the hinges. I set the hinges 3 in. in from the edges of the top (see "Front View" on p. 23).

MAKING THE DRAWER

The drawer is joined at the front with half-blind dovetails and at the rear with a rabbet-and-dado joint. Although half-blind dovetails are a bit more difficult to cut than through dovetails, these are small and few, so the process really doesn't take that much time.

1. Cut the pieces for the drawer front, sides, and back.

2. Mark out the tails on the drawer sides. Begin by scribing a baseline for the tails ⅜-in. back from the front end of each side. Then lay out the tails, spacing them so that the drawer bottom groove will run through a tail, not a pin (see "Lap Desk" on. p. 22).

3. Cut the tails using a small backsaw or bandsaw, and chisel out the waste between them.

4. Lay the tails on the ends of the drawer front and mark the pins by tracing around the tails with a sharp pencil or knife.

5. Use a chisel to remove the waste between the pins (see **photo I**).

Photo I: When removing waste between half-blind pins, make the first cuts around the perimeter of the tail socket and then work down from the top. This will prevent tearout around the sides and bottom of the joint.

6. Test-fit the dovetails, trimming them as necessary to achieve a good fit.

7. Cut the rabbet-and-dado joints at the back of the drawer. Alternatively, you could join the rear of the drawer with through dovetails.

8. Cut the ⅛-in.-wide by ¼-in.-deep groove for the drawer bottom along the inside face of the front and sides.

9. Dry-fit the drawer, then size the bottom to fit its grooves, sliding it in from the back of the drawer. The back edge of the drawer bottom serves as a drawer stop and should project a bit more than ¼ in. from the back of the drawer for right now.

10. Glue up the drawer, making sure it's square and sitting on a flat surface while the glue dries.

11. Attach the drawer bottom to the drawer back with two small screws.

12. Fit the drawer into its opening, sanding or planing it as necessary to achieve a consistent gap around the top and side edges. If the drawer moves sloppily in its opening, you can shim out the sides a bit to get a better fit. If necessary, trim the rear edge of the drawer bottom to allow the face of the drawer to sit flush to the front edges of the box.

13. Finish-sand the drawer, removing any sharp edges.

14. Turn the pull (see "Drawer" on p. 23). Alter-natively, you can buy a wooden pull from many woodworking supply houses (see Sources on p. 145).

FINISHING UP

Because my lap desk was made for use in a kitchen, I wanted to give it a tough finish. I applied several coats of a good-quality water-based lacquer (see **photo J**). Afterward, I buffed it to a soft satin sheen. If the desk were going in any other room, I would probably have used an oil and wax finish, which would look more appropriate for a piece of this type.

Photo J: A water-based polyurethane provides good water and abrasion resistance.

BOOK STAND

The book stand pictured here was made specifically to hold and display a two-volume, handmade Bible, but it could just as easily be used as a dictionary stand or reading stand. For that matter, it could be used as a podium or lectern.

Terry Moore, a furniture maker from Newport, New Hampshire, designed and made this piece. This stand is made of a combination of solid Brazilian rosewood and rosewood veneers, which are accented with hard maple binding and string inlays. The gentle, multiple curves on the legs, the fan-shaped top, and the tripled center stretcher all contribute to a delicate, yet substantial appearance. The stretcher assembly at the bottom holds the four legs stable and square and helps "ground" and balance the stand by keeping it from appearing top heavy.

Although this piece may look complicated, it is actually not that difficult to build. There aren't very many parts and the joinery consists of only a few dowels and biscuits and some mortise-and-tenon joints.

The challenge here lies in the veneer and inlay work, but even that is not beyond the reach of the average woodworker. However, if you feel that the veneer and inlay work may be too much to tackle, you could make the entire piece out of good-quality plywood panels framed with solid wood. And, of course, you don't have to use rosewood; any good-quality hardwood will suffice.

Book Stand

THIS BOOK STAND CAN BE MADE to any height by modifying the leg length. The legs, which flare out in two directions, are bandsawn from solid stock. The top, case top, and case bottom are veneered medium-density fiberboard (MDF) panels, edged with solid wood, and inlayed with strips of maple. The top is edged with maple binding.

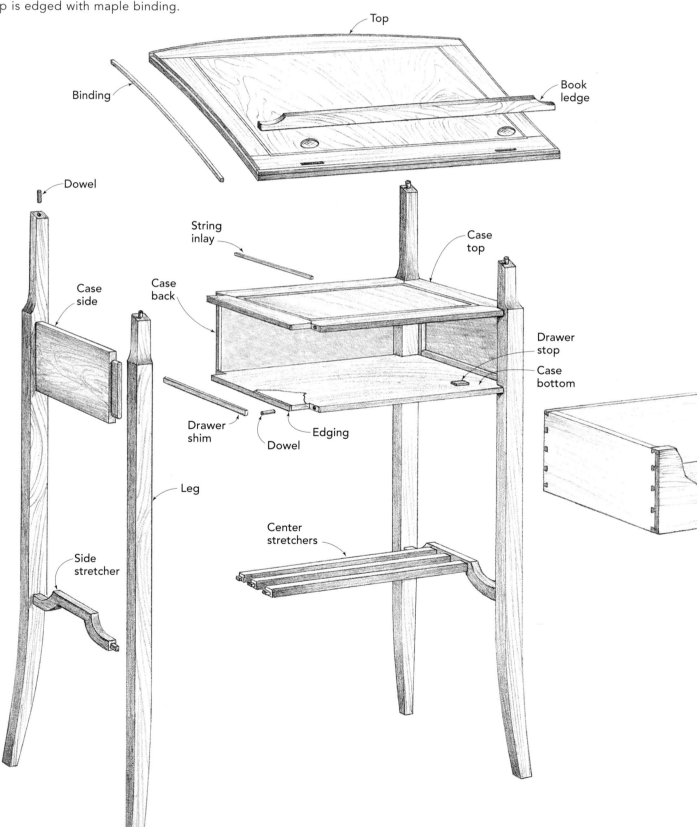

FRONT

SIDE

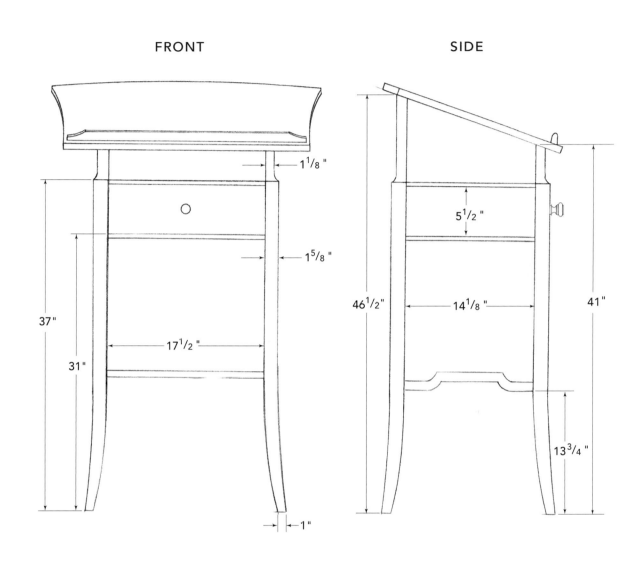

$1^{1}/_{8}$ "

$1^{5}/_{8}$ "

37 "

31 "

$17^{1}/_{2}$ "

1 "

$5^{1}/_{2}$ "

$46^{1}/_{2}$"

$14^{1}/_{8}$ "

41 "

$13^{3}/_{4}$ "

BUILDING THE DESK STEP-BY-STEP

THE BOOK STAND BASICALLY consists of a top and a base. The base includes a three-sided case that which houses a drawer. Build the base before making the top.

(Note: Terry Moore determined the height of his stand by averaging the heights of several different commercially produced podiums. If you are building your book stand for someone above or below average height, you may want to adjust the length of the legs accordingly.)

MAKING THE BASE

Shaping and mortising the legs

1. Make a leg template from stiff cardboard or thin plywood and trace the shape on two adjacent faces of each leg (see "Leg Patterns" on p. 40).

2. Mill the leg blanks to size. Or, if you're making the book stand a different height, cut the legs slightly oversize in length for right now.

3. Cut the legs to shape with a bandsaw. After cutting one profile on each leg, you'll need to either reattach the scrap with tape or redraw the profile on the adjacent face to re-establish your cutting line.

4. Smooth the lower curves with a scraper and the upper radius with a drum sander (see **photo A** on p. 40). The straight sections can be handplaned.

5. Lay out and cut the mortises for the two side stretchers and for the drawer case sides and back (see "Mortise-and-Tenon Details" on p. 41).

6. Finish-sand the legs and set them aside.

Making the stretchers

1. Cut the side stretcher blanks and the center stretchers to the sizes shown.

CUT LIST FOR BOOK STAND		
Base		
2	Leg blanks	2½ in. x 2½ in. x 46¾ in.
2	Leg blanks	2½ in. x 2½ in. x 41¼ in.
2	Side stretchers	¾ in. x 1 in. x 15⅝ in. (including a ⅜-in. x ⅝-in. x ¾-in. tenon on both ends)
3	Center stretchers	¾ in. x 1 in. x 19⅝ in. (including a ⅜-in. x ⅝-in. x ⅝-in. tenon on both ends)
Drawer Case		
2	Sides	¾ in. x 5½ in. x 15⅝ in. (including a ⅜-in. x 4-in. x ¾-in. tenon on both ends)
1	Back	¾ in. x 5½ in. x 19 in. (including a ⅜-in. x 4-in. x ¾-in. tenon on both ends)
1	Top	½ in. x 17¼ in. x 20⅝ in. (including a ⅛-in. edging)
1	Bottom	½ in. x 17¼ in. x 20⅝ in. (including a ⅛-in. edging)
Drawer		
1	Front	¾ in. x 5½ in. x 17 7/16 in.
2	Sides	⅜ in. x 5½ in. x 15 in.
1	Back	⅜ in. x 4 ⅞ in. x 17 7/16 in.
1	Bottom	¼ in. x 14⅞ in. x 17 in.
2	Drawer shims	¾ in. x ¾ in. x 14 in. (planed to final fit)
Top		
1	Top blank	¾ in. x 20¾ in. x 30 in.
1	Book ledge	¾ in. x 1⅛ in. x 26¾ in.
Miscellaneous		
1	Drawer knob	
2	Drawer stops	3/16 in. x ½ in. x 1 in.
12 linear ft.	Maple inlay	1/16 in. x ⅛ in.
10 linear ft.	Maple binding	⅛ in. x ⅛ in.

2. Make a template for the side stretcher pattern, as shown on p. 40, then trace the shape onto the side stretcher blanks. Cut the shape out with a bandsaw or jigsaw.

3. Smooth the side stretchers to final shape using scrapers, files, and a combination of drum and orbital sanders.

4. Chop out the mortises on the inside faces of the two side stretchers and cut the tenons on the end of all five stretchers (see **photo B** on p. 41).

5. Finish-sand all of the parts.

Making the drawer case

The drawer case consists of two sides, a back, a top, and a bottom. The sides and back are made of solid maple veneered on their outside faces with rosewood. The case top and bottom

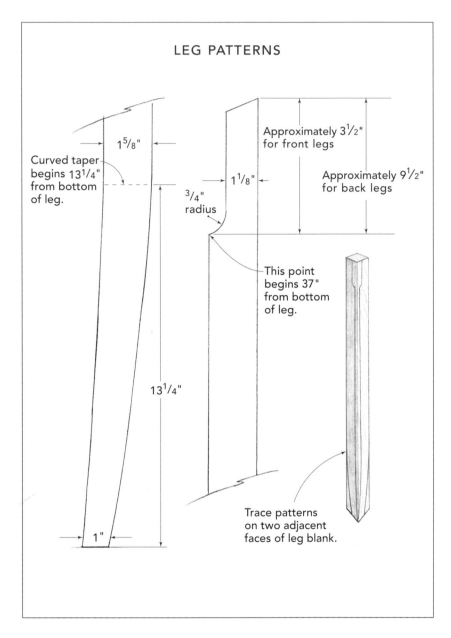

LEG PATTERNS

Curved taper begins 13¼" from bottom of leg.

1⅝"

Approximately 3½" for front legs

1⅛"

Approximately 9½" for back legs

¾" radius

This point begins 37" from bottom of leg.

13¼"

1"

Trace patterns on two adjacent faces of leg blank.

Photo A: A spindle sander is the best way to smooth the radius on the upper portion of the legs.

are made of medium-density fiberboard (MDF) edged with solid wood, then veneered on both faces.

1. Cut the sides and back to size, then glue veneer to one face of each piece, letting the veneer extend a bit over the edges.

2. Clamp the veneer to the case sides by using the sides themselves as cauls. In other words, clamp the sides together with the veneer facing inward. Place wax paper between the veneers as a glue resist. Clamp the veneer to the case back with a similarly sized caul, again using wax paper between the pieces.

3. Once the glue has dried, use a flush-trimming bearing bit in a router to trim the edges of the veneer flush with the sides and end of each piece.

4. Cut the tenons on the drawer box sides and back. Use a sharp, good-quality blade and a slow feed rate to prevent tearout on the face of the veneer.

5. Finish-sand the veneer, being very careful not to cut through the surface. Use a light touch, sanding with a piece of 220-grit paper backed up with a sanding block. If the veneer has deep marks or scratches, you may need to use a scraper to remove them.

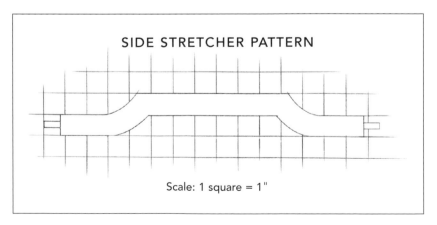

SIDE STRETCHER PATTERN

Scale: 1 square = 1"

MORTISE-AND-TENON DETAILS

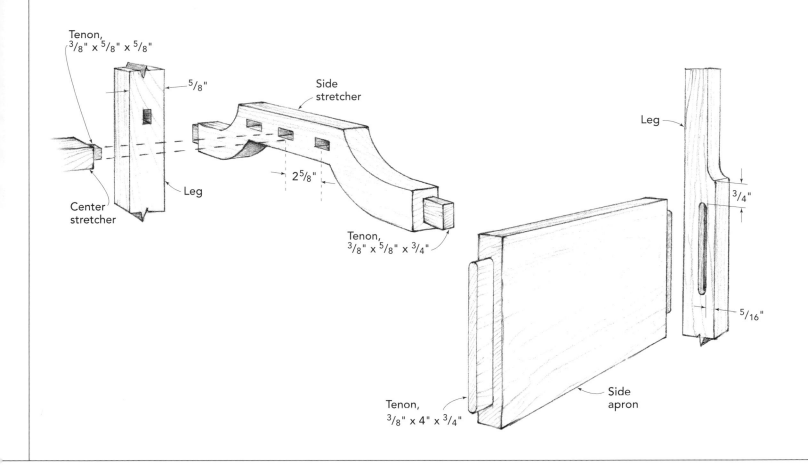

Tenon,
$3/8" \times 5/8" \times 5/8"$

$5/8"$

Center stretcher

Leg

Side stretcher

$2 5/8"$

Tenon,
$3/8" \times 5/8" \times 3/4"$

Leg

$3/4"$

$5/16"$

Tenon,
$3/8" \times 4" \times 3/4"$

Side apron

Photo B: A dado cutter in a table saw works well for sawing tenons on short pieces.

6. Cut two ½-in.-thick MDF panels for the case top and bottom to 17 in. by 20⅝ in., then glue ⅛-in.-thick solid-wood strips around the perimeter of both pieces.

7. After the glue has dried, scrape the edging flush with the faces of the pieces.

8. Veneer both sides of the case bottom, using a single piece of slightly oversize veneer for each. After the glue dries, rout the veneer edges flush to the panel using a flush-trimming bit.

9. Make the veneer assembly for case top (see "Veneering"). Begin by cutting the central field to size (see "Case Top"). Use a straightedge and a sharp knife or veneer saw.

10. Cut border strips to 2⅛ in. wide, miter them, and attach them to the field (see

"Mitering Veneer Borders" on p. 44). Make sure to tape all of the seams on the "show" side of the veneer.

11. Cut a single piece of oversize veneer for the underside of the case top. Then glue it and the top veneer assembly to the case top substrate at the same time (see **photo C** on p. 44).

12. Once the glue is dry, remove the masking tape from the top face of the case top after softening it by touching it lightly with a warm iron set to "wool."

13. Rout the veneer edges flush to the panel.

14. Using a straightedge and a ¹⁄₁₆-in.-diameter spiral router bit, cut a ⅛-in.-deep groove for the maple string inlay around the perimeter of the field veneer (see **photo D** on p. 45). Square up the rounded corners with a small chisel or sharp knife

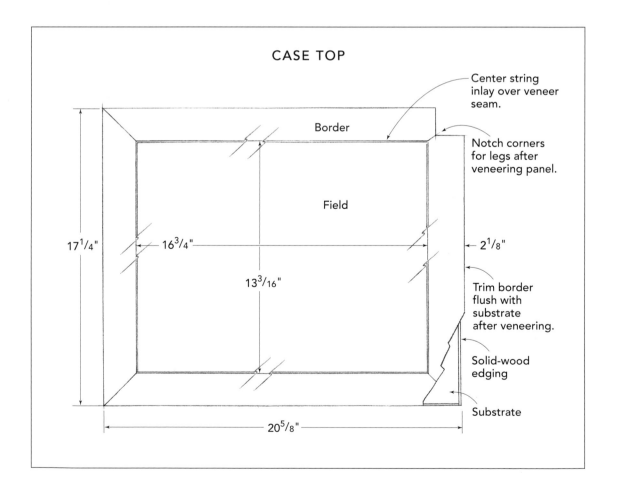

CASE TOP

Center string inlay over veneer seam.

Border

Notch corners for legs after veneering panel.

Field

17¹/₄"

16³/₄"

2¹/₈"

13³/₁₆"

Trim border flush with substrate after veneering.

Solid-wood edging

20⁵/₈"

Substrate

VENEERING

The very thought of attempting the veneer work on this book stand may be somewhat scary. You might think that applying expensive veneers is the domain of highly skilled professional woodworkers—folks who spent years learning the craft and who have vacuum bags, suction pumps, special glues, and other esoteric equipment—but you would be wrong! In fact, the veneer and inlay work on this piece can be done with simple shop tools. All it takes is a little patience, a steady hand, and a willingness to experiment.

Successful veneering depends on a few basic principles: properly selecting and assembling the veneers, choosing an appropriate substrate, carefully gluing the veneers, and cleaning up the finished surfaces. If you haven't veneered before, you might want to experiment on scraps first. And when you start working on your finished piece, veneer the less noticeable parts first, while you get a better feel for the process.

Select and assemble your veneers carefully so that the figure and grain patterns work together harmoniously. If you are veneering a surface with a number of different pieces, join them together before gluing the assembly to the substrate. To join the pieces, first cut the mating edges straight and square, using a knife or sharp veneer saw guided by a straightedge. Then apply glue to the edges, butt them together, and hold them there with masking tape or veneer tape applied to the "show" side of the veneers.

Choose a substrate that is flat, smooth, and free of voids and defects. MDF is an excellent choice because it is flat, dense, very stable, and consistent in thickness. But any good-quality hardwood plywood will also work fine. In general, both sides of the substrate should be veneered, to balance the construction and minimize warping. (This isn't a concern if the piece is fairly small and firmly restrained by sound joinery, like the book stand's case sides and back.) If one face of the workpiece won't be seen, you can cover it with a less expensive grade of veneer.

Apply the veneers after covering the substrate with a consistent, even coat of glue, rolling or brushing it on. Press the veneer into the glue with a hard roller or the side of a glass jar, then firmly clamp the veneer down. Small- or medium-size pieces can be easily clamped between thick panels or cauls. Large pieces may require a vacuum bag or veneer press. It is a good idea to wax the surfaces of the clamping panels or cauls to prevent them from sticking to any glue that may seep through the veneers.

Clean up the veneered surfaces by first removing the tape. Masking tape should be softened first by lightly touching it with a warm iron set to "wool." Pulling off cold tape may tear the veneer or even pull it off the substrate. If you used commercial veneer tape instead, carefully sand it away. After removing the tape, smooth the veneer surfaces using a sharp scraper or 220-grit sandpaper on a sanding block. Never sand with power tools, which can quickly cut through the thin veneers.

MITERING VENEER BORDERS

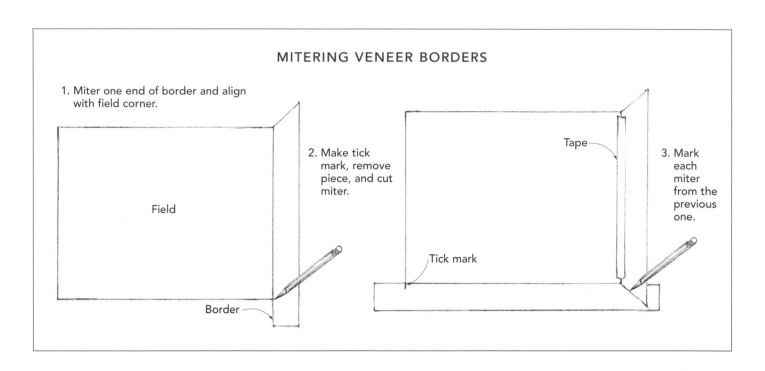

1. Miter one end of border and align with field corner.

Field

Border

2. Make tick mark, remove piece, and cut miter.

Tape

Tick mark

3. Mark each miter from the previous one.

Photo C: Use flat clamping panels and cauls and a lot of clamps to apply the veneer to both sides of a substrate at the same time.

15. Rip enough ⅛-in. by ¹⁄₁₆-in. maple strips for the string inlay. Fit it to its grooves, mitering the ends of the pieces. It should fit snugly enough to require no clamping. Apply a tiny bead of glue in the grooves, then tap the inlay into place with a hammer and block of wood.
16. Carefully scrape and sand the case top flat and smooth.

Gluing up the side assemblies

1. Dry-clamp the legs, stretchers, case sides, and case back together and check the joints for good fits.
2. Clamp a board across the outer side faces of one pair of legs at the height and angle of the top. Trace a line along the board, then cut the two legs to length at the marked angles. Use the first pair of legs as a guide for marking and cutting the opposite pair.
3. Glue up the two side assemblies, joining each case side and side stretcher to its pair of legs. Make sure each assembly is square and flat under clamp pressure. If they are racked or skewed, the stand won't sit flat on the floor and the drawer will be difficult to fit.

Fitting the drawer case top and bottom

1. After the glue has dried, dry-clamp the side assemblies to the case back and center stretchers. Insert and clamp a 17½-in.-long piece of wood between the front legs to square up the entire assembly.
2. Fit the case top and bottom between the legs. The best approach to this is to first make a template from ½-in.-thick plywood. Measure the distances between the legs and mark the corner notches on the template. Cut the template on the table saw, standing the template on end and guiding it with the miter gauge. Set the rip fence to register the width of the cut.

Cut all four notches a bit shy of the cutting lines, then check the fit of the template to the base. If it's a bit too tight, readjust your saw settings and try again. Continue creeping up

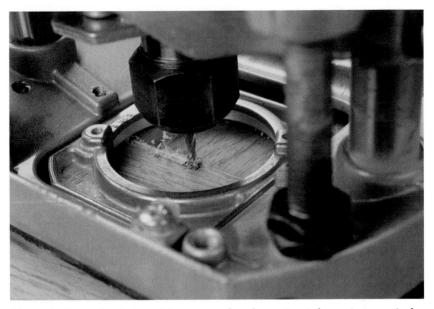

Photo D: Rout the ¹⁄₁₆-in.-wide groove for the string inlay using a spiral bit. Guide the router against a straightedge.

on the cutting line like this until the template fits tightly between the legs. Then use the final table saw settings to cut the case top and bottom.
3. With the case top and bottom in place, extend lines onto the front legs to indicate the position of the top and bottom. Then disassemble the base.
4. Make a doweling jig from a piece of scrap and drill a ¼-in.-diameter by ¾-in.-deep hole into the innermost edge of each front notch and into the adjoining leg (see "A Doweling Jig" on p. 46). The dowels stabilize the front edges of the case top and bottom.
5. Cut two ¼-in.-diameter dowels to a length of 1⅜ in. and set them aside for now.

Completing the base assembly

1. Lay one side assembly on your workbench and glue one end of the case back and one end of each of the center stretchers in place.
2. Glue the dowels into their holes in the case top and bottom.
3. Spread glue along the edges of the case side and back, then insert the case bottom and top into place on the leg assembly.

Tip: Small gaps between the string inlay and the surrounding dark veneer can be rendered nearly invisible by filling them with a mixture of powdered graphite and epoxy.

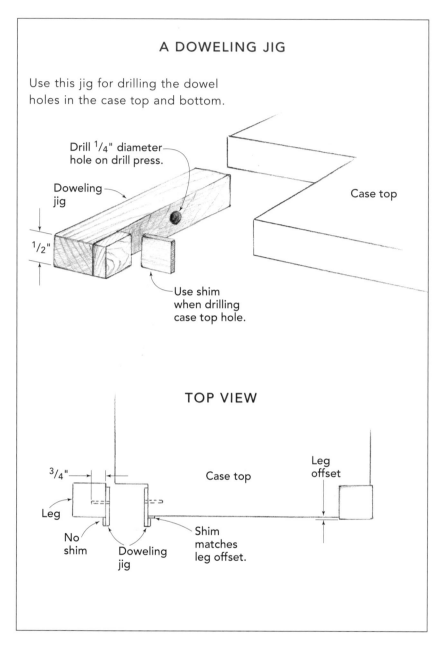

A DOWELING JIG

Use this jig for drilling the dowel holes in the case top and bottom.

Drill $1/4$" diameter hole on drill press.

Doweling jig

$1/2$"

Use shim when drilling case top hole.

Case top

TOP VIEW

$3/4$"

Leg offset

Case top

Leg

No shim

Doweling jig

Shim matches leg offset.

Tip: To correct unequal footing, shim the assembly steady on a flat surface and use one thin piece of scrap to gauge a scribe line onto each leg. Then saw to the gauge line.

Photo E: The book-matched field on the top is set off from the border pieces with a thin framework of maple string inlay. Strips of ⅛-in.-wide maple binding wrap around the outer edges of the top.

4. Spread glue on the edges of the remaining case side and into the mortises on the legs, then attach the second side assembly.

5. Stand the assembled unit up on a flat surface and clamp all of the parts together, making sure that the assembly is square and that it stands solidly.

MAKING THE TOP

The top is a piece of veneered ¾-in.-thick MDF trimmed with solid-wood edging. The book-matched central field is set off from the border pieces with a thin framework of maple string inlay. Strips of ⅛-in.-wide maple binding wrap around the outer edges of the top (see **photo E**). Although the veneer and inlay work may look complicated, it is actually quite easy.

Preparing the substrate

1. Make a stiff paper half-pattern template for the top using the pattern shown in "Top Detail."

2. Cut a piece of ¾-in.-thick MDF to about 22 in. by 31 in.; then, using your paper template, trace the shape of the top onto the MDF.

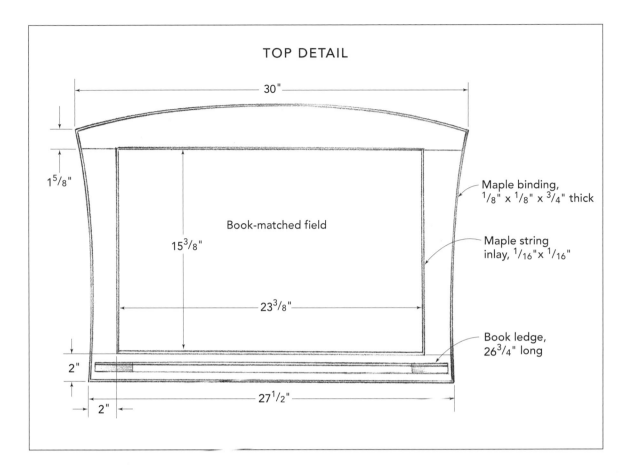

TOP DETAIL

30"

1⁵/₈"

Book-matched field

15³/₈"

23³/₈"

Maple binding,
¹/₈" x ¹/₈" x ³/₄" thick

Maple string
inlay, ¹/₁₆" x ¹/₁₆"

Book ledge,
26³/₄" long

2"

27¹/₂"

2"

3. Cut the top to shape with a bandsaw, then sand the edges smooth.

4. Rip four ⅛-in.-thick strips of solid wood for the edging. Make the strips a bit wider than ¾ in.

5. Fit the edging to the top, mitering the pieces at their corners. Then glue and clamp them in place (see **photo F**).

6. Once the glue has dried, use a scraper to carefully shave the edging flush to the faces of the MDF panel.

Constructing the veneer assembly

The easiest way to accurately lay out the pieces for the veneer assembly is to make a veneering template that is the exact size and

Photo F: Before gluing veneer to the book stand top, apply the ⅛-in.-thick solid-wood edging, mitering it at the corners.

Photo G: Before applying a composition of veneers to a substrate, glue the pieces together at their edges, holding them in place with tape placed on the show side of the veneers.

shape as the top. It will help you lay out the veneer components and trim the taped-up assembly to size before gluing it to the top.

1. Make the veneering template from ¼-in.-thick hardboard. You can quickly rout it to shape by temporarily attaching your template blank to the top substrate and then following the shape of the substrate with a flush-trimming bit.

2. Mark the size and shape of the five veneer components directly onto the template (see "Top Detail" on p. 47). Extend the veneer seamlines down the edge of the template.

3. Make the field from two pieces of book-matched veneers (see Sources on p. 145). Cut the adjoining edges with a sharp utility knife and a straightedge. Make the pieces about ¼ in. oversize for right now.

4. Glue the two halves of the field together. Apply a thin bead of glue to the mating edges, butt them together tightly, and connect them with a wide strip of masking tape applied to the show side of the veneers.

5. Once the glue has dried, lay the field on your template and knife it to final width using a straightedge placed on the template's veneer seam reference lines. Leave it oversize in height for right now.

6. Cut oversize pieces of veneer for the side border pieces, then attach them to the edges of the field with glue and tape.

7. Knife the top and bottom edges of the field and side border assembly to create a total height of 15⅜ in. Use a straightedge to guide your knife and make sure the cuts are perpendicular to the sides of the field.

8. Cut oversize pieces of veneer for the top and bottom borders. Glue and tape one straight edge of each piece to the field and side border assembly. Let the assembly dry (see **photo G**).

9. Lay the veneer assembly glue side up on your bench. Draw a vertical centerline from top to bottom, bisecting the field.

10. Lay the template on the veneer. Align the reference lines on the edges of the template with the veneer's centerline. Then align the top and bottom border seams with the reference marks on the side edges of the template.

11. Using the edges of the template as a guide, knife the veneer to the shape of the template (see **photo H**).

12. Using the template, knife a single piece of veneer for the underside of the top.

Applying the veneer, binding, and string inlay

1. Glue and clamp the veneer to the top and bottom of the substrate at the same time, using two thick, flat scrap panels as cauls. It's a good idea to wax the faces of the cauls first to prevent glue squeeze-out from sticking to them.

2. After the glue has dried thoroughly, remove the tape with a warm iron, as before. Then clean up the veneer surfaces with a scraper and 220-grit sandpaper, using a very light touch, especially near the corners. Avoid power sanding, which can quickly cut through the thin veneers.

3. Rout a ⅛-in. by ⅛-in. rabbet around the edges of the entire panel to accept the maple binding.

4. Rip ⅛-in.-square strips of maple for the binding, then fit them into the rabbets, mitering them at their corners. Glue them in place, clamping them into the rabbets with tightly stretched tape.

5. Install the string inlay around the perimeter of the field in the same manner as you did for the case top.

6. Use a scraper to trim the inlay flush with the veneer and round over the edges of the binding slightly with 220-grit sandpaper.

7. Make the book ledge (see "Book Ledge Detail"). Then glue it to the top with five or six #20 biscuits, centering the ledge within the bottom veneer border.

Photo H: Use a hardboard template to trim the top veneer assembly to shape.

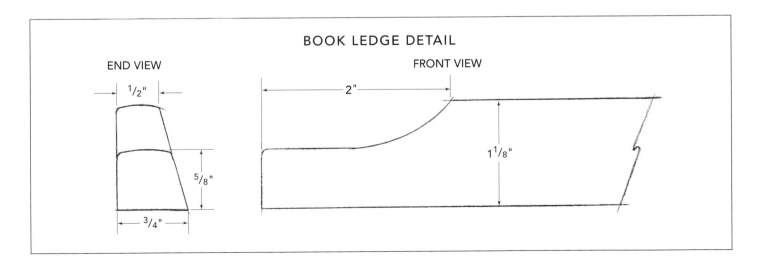

BOOK LEDGE DETAIL

END VIEW

FRONT VIEW

1/2"

2"

5/8"

1 1/8"

3/4"

Attaching the top

The book stand top is attached to the legs with dowels (see "Book Stand" on p. 36). Installing the dowels into the legs at the proper angle and then drilling the corresponding angled holes in the underside of the top may seem a bit tricky, but the tasks are quite easy with the use of a jig.

1. To make the jig, begin by cutting a piece of 1⅛-in.-square scrap stock to a length of about 2 in.

2. Locate the axis of the stock by drawing diagonal lines across each end. Then drill a ⅜-in.-diameter hole straight down through the center of the piece using the drill press.

3. Cut one end of the jig at an angle complementary to the angle at the top of the legs, so that the walls of the jig are parallel to the walls of the leg (see **photo I**).

4. Attach a piece of sandpaper to the angled end of the jig with spray adhesive or double-sided tape. The sandpaper will help keep the jig from slipping as you drill the dowel holes.

5. Drill a dowel hole in the end of each leg. Place the angled end of the jig on top of a leg, and drill down about 1 in. Hold the jig tightly, making sure it stays aligned with the edges of the leg while you're drilling.

6. Lay the top upside down on a bench and center the base on it. Lightly trace the outline of the legs onto the top with a pencil. Make your marks precise, because even small errors here can affect the fit of the top.

7. Remove the base and use the jig to drill the dowel holes in the top. Place the jig, angled side down, within your traced lines. Make sure the jig is angled in the correct direction, then hold it firmly and drill the dowel holes about ½ in. deep (see **photo J**). Be very careful not to drill through the top!

8. Insert a 1½-in.-long dowel into each hole in the top, then test-fit the top to the base. The dowels in the top should slide into the holes

Photo I: To drill the dowel holes in the legs, use a jig that is cut to a complementary angle to that of the legs. Sandpaper on the face of the jig helps keep it in place when drilling.

Photo J: After tracing the leg locations on the underside of the top panel, use the same drilling jig to bore the holes in the panel.

in the legs with just a few whacks of your hand. If the holes are very slightly misaligned, use a file to put a slight chamfer along the opening of each leg hole. This chamfer will act as a funnel to guide the dowels home. If the dowels simply won't line up properly, you may have to plug one or more of the holes in the top and redrill them.

9. When the top fits well, glue the dowels into the top holes, then glue the top in place.

MAKING THE DRAWER

The drawer on Moore's piece was designed to store a Bible, but it could also be used to hold pens, pencils, and paper. Moore made his drawer sides, back, and bottom from solid mahogany. The drawer front is a piece of walnut faced with rosewood veneer (see **photo K**). Half-blind dovetails attach the front to the drawer sides. The rear joints are through dovetails.

1. Dimension the front, sides, and back of the drawer box.

2. Lay out and cut the tails on both ends of the sides (see "Drawer Details" on p. 52).

3. Lay the tails in place onto the edges of the drawer front and back and trace their outlines to lay out the pins.

4. Saw the shoulders of the pins and chisel out the waste between them. (For more on dovetailing, see Lap Desk (p. 20).

5. Cut a ³⁄₁₆-in.-deep by ¼-in.-wide groove into the sides and front to accept the drawer bottom. This is easily done on the table saw using a dado cutter.

6. Dry-fit the parts and measure for a bottom that will fit snugly between the side grooves, then make the bottom. Although Moore's drawer bottom is solid mahogany, you could just as easily use ¼-in.-thick plywood, which I prefer because it won't expand and contract. If you do use solid wood, make sure the grain runs parallel to the drawer front.

Photo K: The sides, back, and bottom of this drawer are solid mahogany. The drawer front is walnut faced with a rosewood veneer.

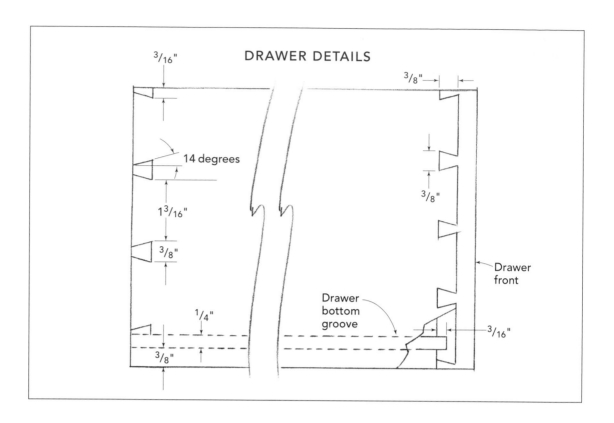

DRAWER DETAILS

3/16"

14 degrees

1 3/16"

3/8"

1/4"

3/8"

3/8"

3/8"

Drawer
front

Drawer
bottom
groove

3/16"

Photo L: When installing a solid-wood drawer bottom, allow for wood movement by cutting slots for the screws.

7. Glue up the drawer, making sure that it is flat and square, then slide the bottom, unglued, into its grooves. If you use plywood for the bottom, simply attach it to the back of the drawer with a few screws. If you made a solid-wood panel, first cut a slot for each screw so the wood can expand and contract (see **photo L**).

8. If you are making your own drawer pull, now is the time to turn it (see "Drawer Pull Detail").

Installing the drawer shims and stops

1. Check the fit of the drawer in its opening. Then plane the top and bottom edges of the drawer to create an all-around clearance of about ½₂ in.

2. Shim out the inside of the case so the drawer doesn't twist or rack when it is opened and closed (see "Book Stand" on p. 36). Begin by making the shims so that they project about ½₂ in. into the drawer opening. Plane them as necessary to allow the drawer to slide easily, then glue them to the sides of the case.

3. Make the ³⁄₁₆-in.-thick by ½-in.-wide by 1-in.-long drawer stops from scrap wood (see "Book Stand" on p. 36). The stops get installed to the case bottom just behind the drawer front.

4. To initially position the stops, draw two gauge lines on the case bottom, each about ¾ in. back from the front edge of the case bottom and about 2 in. in from the legs.

5. Coat one face of each stop with some quick-setting epoxy and then place the stops on the case bottom with their front edges even with the gauge lines.

6. Slide the drawer into its opening, gently pushing it in ½₆ in. past the front edge of the case bottom. This will push the stops back a tiny bit into their proper positions. It is wise to coat the bottom and back edges of the drawer front with wax to prevent it from sticking to any epoxy squeeze-out. Leave the drawer in position until the epoxy cures.

7. Finish-sand the drawer, then install the pull with a screw from inside the drawer front.

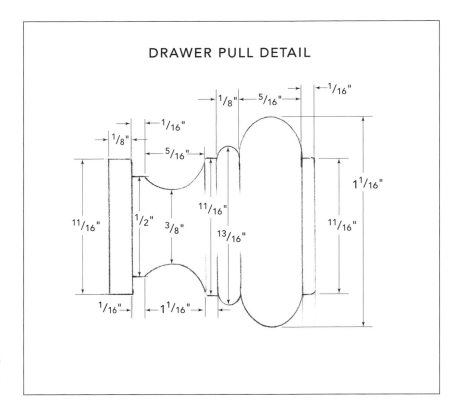

DRAWER PULL DETAIL

FINISHING UP

Moore applied several coats of gloss nitrocellulose lacquer to accentuate the rich color and grain of the rosewood. He then rubbed out the finish to a high shine. But if you don't have access to spray equipment, you should be able to get a warm, polished look with a good-quality brush- or wipe-on finish.

The sides and bottom of Moore's drawer are coated with lemon-scented wax. The wax not only protects the wood and helps the drawer slide freely but also surprises you with a pleasant lemon fragrance when the drawer is opened.

LAPTOP DESK

Stephen Lauziere, who designed this desk, faced an interesting problem. His customer, a writer, wanted a piece of furniture that could serve as a laptop computer desk by day and a living room table by night. Lauziere's problem stemmed from the fact that normal table height is 29 in. to 30 in., whereas the ideal height for a computer keyboard is much lower, at about 26 in.

The obvious solution was to place the computer in a drawer below the desktop so it could be pulled out when needed and tucked away out of sight when not being used. But putting the computer in a drawer would mean that the user's hands would have to hang over the drawer front to type on the keyboard. This would be awkward, uncomfortable, and stressful on the wrists. Lauziere solved the problem by building a slide-out tray that hides behind a drawer front. When the tray is closed, it looks like a regular drawer. But when opened, the drawer front folds down flush with the tray, creating a flat, easily accessible work area.

This desk is practical and sturdy, yet light and elegant in design. The curved, tapered legs and slide-out tray may make the desk appear complicated, but it is actually a relatively easy project to build. The desk is assembled with basic mortise-and-tenon joinery and with a few dadoes and rabbets.

Laptop Desk

TO GIVE SUPPORT TO THE SLIDE-OUT TRAY, an upper and lower inner frame hold vertical support pieces. The tray slides in grooves cut in the vertical supports. The four skirts are glued to the four legs and then the lower inner frame is glued to grooves cut in the bottom of the back and side skirts. After the vertical supports are slid into place and glued, the upper inner frame is glued to the grooves in the top of the three skirts.

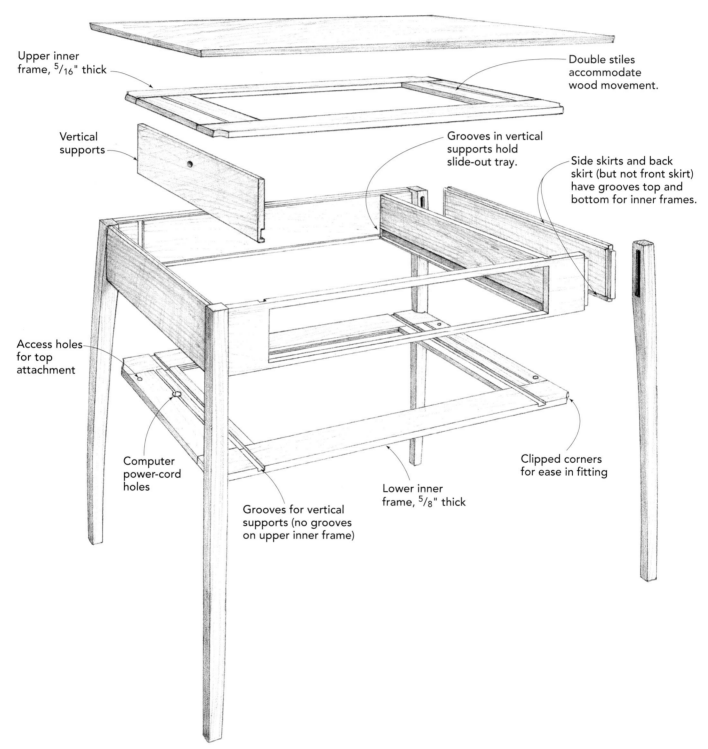

Upper inner frame, $5/16$" thick

Double stiles accommodate wood movement.

Vertical supports

Grooves in vertical supports hold slide-out tray.

Side skirts and back skirt (but not front skirt) have grooves top and bottom for inner frames.

Access holes for top attachment

Computer power-cord holes

Grooves for vertical supports (no grooves on upper inner frame)

Lower inner frame, $5/8$" thick

Clipped corners for ease in fitting

SIDE VIEW

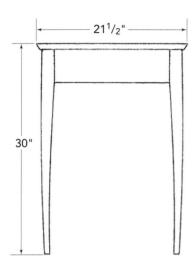

21$^{1}/_{2}$"

30"

FRONT VIEW

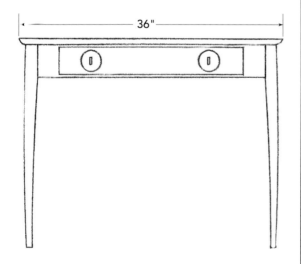

36"

CUT LIST FOR LAPTOP DESK

1	Top	¾ in. x 21½ in. x 36 in.
Base		
4	Legs	1⅜ in. x 1⅜ in. x 29¼ in.
2	Side skirts	¾ in. x 4⅝ in. x 18¾ in. (including a ¼-in. x ⅝-in. x 3⅜-in. tenon on both ends)
1	Front skirt	¾ in. x 4⅝ in. x 32¾ in. (including a ¼-in. x ⅝-in. x 3⅜-in. tenon on both ends)
1	Back skirt	¾ in. x 4⅝ in. x 32¾ in. (including a ¼-in. x ⅝-in. x 3⅜-in. tenon on both ends)
Inner Framework		
2	Vertical supports	¾ in. x 3¹⁵⁄₁₆ in. x 19 in.
2	Lower frame rails	⅝ in. x 2¼ in. x 33 in.
4	Lower frame stiles	⅝ in. x 2¼ in. x 15¼ in. (including a ¼-in. x ½-in. x 2¼-in. tenon on both ends)
2	Upper frame rails	⁵⁄₁₆ in. x 2¼ in. x 33 in.
4	Upper frame stiles	⁵⁄₁₆ in. x 2¼ in. x 15¼ in. (including a ⅛-in. x ½-in. x 2¼-in. tenon on both ends)
Slide-Out Tray		
1	Back rail	1 in. x 2¼ in. x 25 in.
3	Stiles	1 in. x 2¼ in. x 17⅛ in. (including a ¼-in. x 1-in. x 1⅜-in. tenon on one end and a ³⁄₁₆-in. x 3½-in. tongue on other end)
2	Front rails	1 in. x 2¼ in. x 11⅛ in. (including a ¼-in. x 1-in. x 1⅜-in. tenon on both ends)
1	Subrail	⅜ in. x 3½ in. x 25 in.
2	Panels	½ in. x 9⅝ in. x 10⅞ in. (including a ¼-in. x ¼-in. tongue on all sides)
1	Drawer front	¾ in. x 3⅝ in. x 25⅝ in.
Miscellaneous		
2	Drawer runners	³⁄₁₆ in. x 1¹⁄₁₆ in. x 18⅝ in.
1	Back stop strip	¼ in. x 1⁵⁄₁₆ in. x 24⅞ in.
2	Stop blocks	¼ in. x ½ in. x 2 in.

Slide-Out Tray

THE DRAWER FRONT FOLDS DOWN FLUSH with the slide-out panel to become part of the computer work surface. The drawer front rests on stiles that extend past the rails of the frame-and-panel slide-out tray. A thin subrail is half-lapped on top of the extended rails. A strip, attached to the back of the tray, stops against blocks screwed to the vertical supports.

SLIDE-OUT TRAY CONSTRUCTION

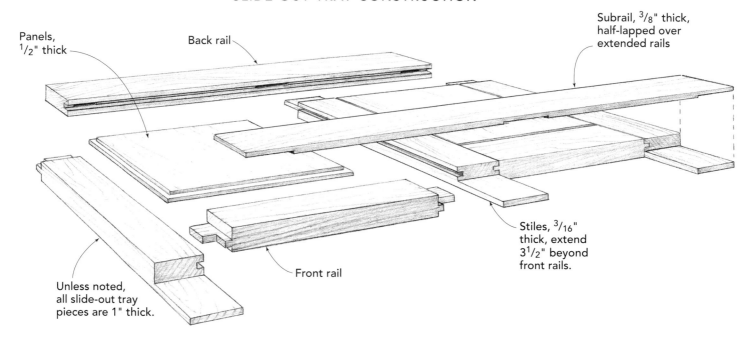

Panels, $^1/_2$" thick

Back rail

Subrail, $^3/_8$" thick, half-lapped over extended rails

Stiles, $^3/_{16}$" thick, extend $3^1/_2$" beyond front rails.

Front rail

Unless noted, all slide-out tray pieces are 1" thick.

SLIDE-OUT TRAY INSTALLED

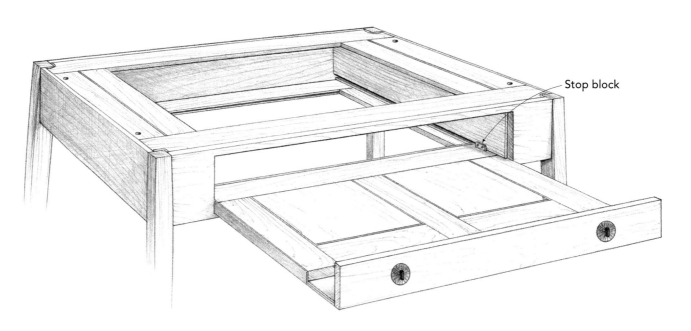

Stop block

TRAY RUNNERS AND STOP STRIP

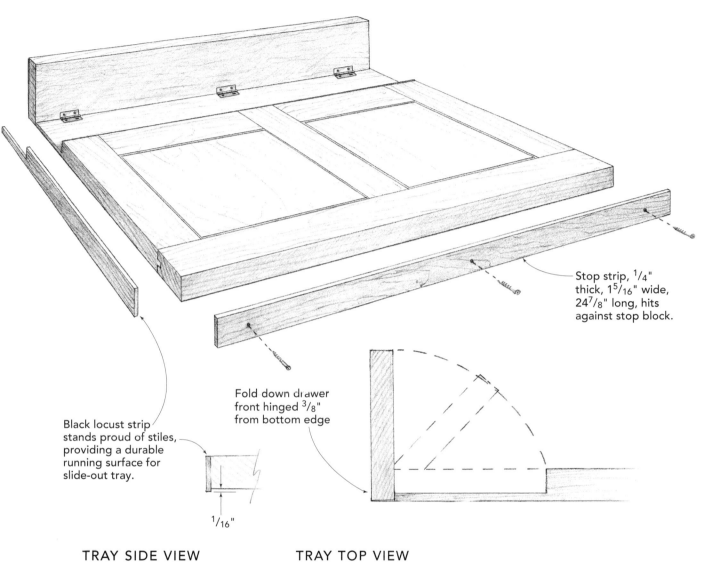

Stop strip, $^1/_4$" thick, $1^5/_{16}$" wide, $24^7/_8$" long, hits against stop block.

Fold down drawer front hinged $^3/_8$" from bottom edge

Black locust strip stands proud of stiles, providing a durable running surface for slide-out tray.

$^1/_{16}$"

TRAY SIDE VIEW   TRAY TOP VIEW

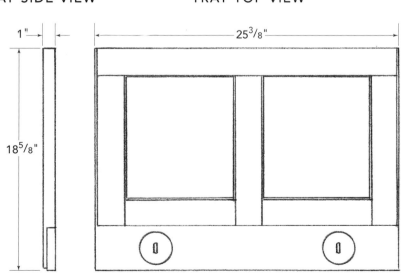

1"

$25^3/_8$"

$18^5/_8$"

BUILDING THE DESK STEP-BY-STEP

THE LAPTOP DESK can be broken down into four basic components: the top, the base, the inner framework, and the slide-out tray. Begin by making the top, then make the parts for the base. Next, make the inner framework, then assemble it along with the base. Last, make the sliding tray and fit it into its opening.

MAKING THE TOP

The top is the most visible part of the desk, so select your straightest, best-looking stock for it, laying out the boards for good color and grain match.

1. Mill enough stock for the top to make it 2 in. oversize in length, and 1 in. oversize in width.

2. Edge glue the boards, making sure the resulting plank is flat under clamp pressure (see **photo A**).

Photo B: After sawing the bevels on the edges of the top, smooth the cut and round the edges using a block plane.

Photo A: Edge glue the boards for the top, alternating the clamps over and under to help prevent the panel from springing under clamp pressure.

3. Surface both sides of the top smooth and flat with a belt sander, plane, scraper, or a combination of the three.

4. Cut the top to size by ripping it to width and crosscutting it to length.

5. Saw or plane a 30-degree bevel on the edges of the top to give it a lighter and more delicate look. Then round over the edges slightly with a plane and some sandpaper (see **photo B**).

6. Finish-sand the entire top.

MAKING THE BASE

The base consists primarily of the legs and skirts, which connect with mortise-and-tenon joinery. When making the skirts, you must also cut the joints for attaching the inner framework. Note that the drawer front is cut from the center of the front skirt to maintain grain continuity across the front of the desk.

Shaping the legs

Each leg is tapered and curved on all four faces. On the two outside faces, the curve begins at the top of the leg, and on the two inside faces, the curve starts 5 in. down from the top.

1. Mill the stock for the legs. Although the finished dimension at the top of the legs is only 1⅜ in. by 1⅜ in., you will need to start with 2-in.-square blanks to leave enough thickness to cut the curves.

2. Determine how each leg will be positioned and clearly mark the ends. This will prevent possible confusion later when laying out the curves.

3. Lay out and cut the mortises on the two inside faces of each leg. Inset each mortise ⅜ in. from the inside corner of the leg (see "Laptop Desk" on p. 56).

4. Make a heavy cardboard or thin wood pattern for laying out the curves on the legs (see "Leg Pattern").

5. Use the pattern to lay out the curves on all of the faces of each leg.

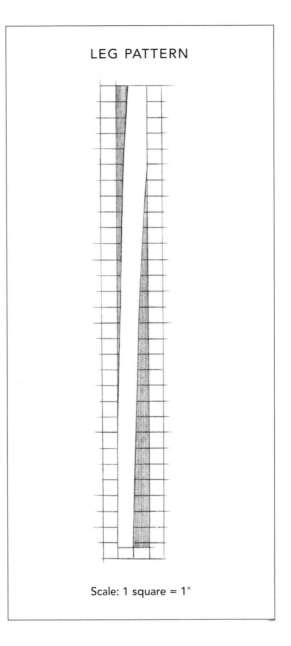

LEG PATTERN

Scale: 1 square = 1"

6. To shape each leg, begin by sawing one outside curve (see **photo C** on p. 62). Next, position the other outside face of the leg facing upward, and use your template to retrace the section of the curve that you just sawed away. Then make that cut.

7. Plane, scrape, or sand the outside faces to create a smooth surface for the workpiece to ride on when making the inside face cuts.

8. Saw the inside faces of the legs, again retracing the curves as necessary after cutting away part of an adjacent face (see **photo D** on p. 62).

Photo C: When cutting the leg curves, saw a bit shy of the cut line, leaving the remaining waste to be cleaned up with hand tools.

9. Clean up the inside faces using a compass plane, spokeshave, scraper, or belt sander (see photo E).

Making the skirt

1. Dimension the side and back skirts, remembering to include the necessary length for the tenon on each end.

2. Mill one board that will be used for both the front skirt and the drawer front. Make the workpiece ¼ in. wider than given to allow for the saw kerf waste created when ripping the skirt into three pieces, as described next.

3. Rip a ⅝-in.-wide strip off the bottom edge of the board and a 5/16-in.-wide strip off the top edge.

4. Crosscut 3 in. off of each end of the center ripping. These will be reglued onto the skirt. Set the remainder of the center ripping aside; it will later be used for the drawer front.

5. Make the front skirt by gluing the 3-in.-long ends between the top and bottom rippings. Carefully align the pieces in their original positions at the outermost ends of the skirt. Let the glue dry thoroughly.

Photo D: After cutting each face of the leg, align the template with the remaining portion of the original line on the adjacent face and retrace the shape.

Photo E: I use a
scraper to smooth
the saw marks from
the bandsawn leg.

6. Lay out and cut the tenons on the ends of
the skirts, mitering their ends to meet inside
the legs. Make sure the tenons fit snugly in
their mortises.

7. Cut the rabbets in the top and bottom
edges of the back and side skirts. The front
skirt does not get rabbets.

8. Cut the ¾-in.-wide by ¼-in.-deep dadoes in
the front and back skirts that hold the vertical
supports.

9. Finish-sand the skirts.

BUILDING THE INNER FRAMEWORK

The inner framework consists of an upper and
lower frame and two vertical supports. Both
frames provide strength and stability to the
base, while the upper frame serves double-
duty as an attachment for the desktop.

Grooves in the vertical supports provide the
bearing surface for the sliding tray.

1. Dimension the two vertical supports, the
four long rails, and the eight short stiles.
Double stiles are used instead of a single wide
stile to minimize wood movement problems
(see **photo F** on p. 64).

2. Rip the ¼-in.-wide by ½-in.-deep grooves in
the inside edges of the rails, then cut tenons
on the stiles to fit.

3. Glue up the frames, making sure they are
absolutely square (see **photo G** on p. 64).

4. Sand the frames flat and smooth. Because
you won't see them, you don't have to go
overboard, but I generally ease all sharp edges
and remove any rough spots.

5. Saw the 1-in.-wide by ¼-in.-deep grooves in
the vertical supports that will hold the slide-
out tray. Space the grooves ¼ in. up from the
bottom edge of the supports. Also, cut the

Photo F: Doubled-up stiles on the inner frames prevent the wood movement problems you might experience with a single wide stile.

¾-in.-wide by ¼-in.-deep grooves in the lower frame that house the vertical supports.

6. Sand the grooves in the vertical supports to ensure smooth movement of the slide-out tray.

7. Drill four screw holes in the upper frame for attaching the top (see "Laptop Desk" on p. 56). Elongate the holes with a round file to allow for cross-grain expansion and contraction of the solid-wood top.

8. Drill four large holes in the lower frame, aligning them with the screw holes in the top frame. These large holes are for screwdriver access when attaching the top. I made mine ¾ in. in diameter to give myself a little "wiggle room."

9. Drill a 1½-in.-diameter hole in the vertical support and one in the lower frame for passage of electrical plugs.

Photo G: To pull a freshly glued assembly into square, squeeze a clamp across opposite corners until opposing diagonal measurements match.

Assembling the Desk

I assembled the base and top before making the slide-out tray so I could be sure the tray fit perfectly.

1. Glue the legs and skirts together. Be sure the base assembly is square, or you will run into problems fitting the inner framework.

2. After the leg-and-skirt assembly has been unclamped, glue the lower frame into the rabbets in the back and side skirts. (You will have to notch the corners of the frames to fit around the legs.) Be sure the grooves for the vertical supports line up with the dadoes in the front and back skirts.

3. Apply glue to the dadoes in the skirts and lower frame, then slide the vertical supports into place. Make sure the bottom edges of the grooves in the vertical supports are slightly higher than the opening in the front skirt, otherwise the slide-out tray won't operate properly.

4. Glue the upper frame into its rabbets in the top edges of the back and side skirts.

5. Clean up any glue squeeze-out and give everything a light sanding. Then set the assembly aside while you build the slide-out tray.

Building the Slide-Out Tray

The slide-out tray is a frame-and-panel assembly that's actually built more like a door than a drawer. It consists of stiles, rails, and floating panels. The frame members connect with mortise-and-tenon joints, and the panels float unglued in grooves in the frame. The drawer front is hinged to the front edge of the tray.

1. Make the two floating panels, gluing up several boards if necessary to get the width that you need. The dimensions for the panels given are somewhat tight, so expect to trim them to fit after making the frame.

2. Dimension the back and front rails, the subrail, and the three stiles, making sure to include the length of the tenons on one end of each stile.

3. Cut the mortises in the back rail and all of the stiles. Then rip a ¼-in.-wide by ⅜-in.-deep groove in the inside edges of rails and stiles. The bottom edge of the groove should sit ½ in. down from the upper faces of the frame members to align the top face of the ½-in.-thick panels flush with the top face of the frame.

4. Cut the tenons on the back end of each stile and both ends of the two rails. Make sure they fit snugly in their mortises.

5. Use a dado head to cut down the front end of the three stiles to 3⁄16 in. thick. The cut should end 3½ in. from the end of each stile.

6. Cut the three 3⁄16-in.-deep half laps in the subrail.

7. Dry-fit the frames and measure for the two panels.

8. Cut the panels to width and length, allowing for wood movement (see "Dealing with Wood Movement" on p. 13). After squaring the panels, cut the ¼-in.-deep by ⅜-in.-wide rabbets on the top side to create the ¼-in.-thick tongues that fit in the frame grooves.

9. Glue up the entire tray, making sure the assembly remains square and flat under clamp pressure.

10. After the glue dries, attach the subrail and then sand the entire assembly smooth and flat.

11. Hinge the drawer front to the front of the tray. Begin by mortising the hinges into the subrail. Then align the bottom edge of drawer front with the bottom face of the subrail and mark out the mortises in the back of the drawer front. After cutting the mortises, attach the drawer front, making sure it folds down flush with the top face of the sliding tray (see **photo H** on p. 66).

12. Attach two hard-wearing wood strips to the sides of the tray to minimize sliding fric-

Photo H: The drawer front folds down flush with the tray to create a flat working surface. The recessed pulls won't interfere with your hands or the computer.

tion and to protect the tray sides from wear. Locust, hickory, and white oak are all good choices. Make the pieces ⅟₁₆ in. wider than the thickness of the tray and attach them with the overhang projecting off the bottom of the tray.

13. Screw a ¼-in.-thick by 1³⁄₁₆-in.-wide strip to the back edge of the tray to serve as a stop strip. The strip will bump against stop blocks on the vertical supports to prevent the tray from falling out.

14. To install the stop blocks, first insert the tray a few inches into its grooves. Then place the stop block against the rear stop strip and against each vertical support, then drill for the stop block screws. You'll fasten the stop blocks after finishing the desk and installing the tray.

Making the pulls

The pulls are T-shaped pieces of walnut mortised into a carved recess (see "Pull" on p. 69). The recess is easy to make, even for someone with little or no carving experience.

1. Draw two 2¾-in.-diameter circles on the drawer front to establish the perimeter of each finished recess.

2. To provide a depth reference and to remove the bulk of the waste, drill a ⁵⁄₁₆-in.-deep hole in center of the pull area using a ⅞-in.-diameter Forstner bit (see **photo I**).

3. Begin shaping the recess with a large gouge, cutting inward from the perimeter (see **photo J**).

4. Once the recess is roughed out to its approximate shape, finish off the carving with a narrow veining tool (see **photo K**).

Photo I: To establish the perimeter and depth of the pull recess, draw its outer diameter, then drill a flat-bottomed hole in the center.

Photo J: Rough out the recess with a gouge, carving from the perimeter inward.

Photo K: Use a veining tool to texture the recess, spacing the cuts evenly around the circle.

GLUING UP LARGE PANELS

To minimize chances of a desktop or other large panel warping, I generally don't make the panel from boards wider than about 6 in. Whenever possible, I also reverse the growth rings on adjacent boards (see "Minimizing Panel Warpage"). However, the color and figure of the boards ultimately dictate how they will be arranged. For example, if I have an attractive board that is wide and flat, I may use it as one piece rather than ripping it up and ruining the figure. Or if the back of a board contains sapwood, I won't flip the board over simply to reverse the growth rings. After arranging boards for a panel, I draw a continuous, light pencil line across their faces for placement reference during glue-up.

I generally straighten and square up the edges of a board on a jointer. I find that a well-tuned jointer squares edges better than a handplane in a fraction of the time. If your jointer fence isn't perfectly square to the table, you can cancel out the resulting angles by alternating opposite faces of adjacent boards against the jointer fence.

It's wise to dry-clamp a panel to check for a tight edge joint before applying glue. If you have to really crank the clamps to pull the boards together, then the edges need to be reworked so they don't pull apart over time from the built-in stress. Remove the boards in question and joint them again until they meet without gaps. For bowed or very long boards, I sometimes use biscuits, dowels, or a machined glue joint to help align the edges.

When clamping, alternate the clamps over and under the panel to ensure even pressure and to keep the panel from springing. If the edges of the boards don't quite line up, loosen the clamps a bit, and rap the boards with a rubber mallet (see photo A on p. 60). Once the boards are aligned, tighten the clamps firmly, but not so hard that you crush the wood. The joints should be tight along their entire length and a small bead of glue should squeeze out from each side. It's best to remove glue squeeze-out before it cures, because scraping off hardened glue tends to tear out bits of wood. You can wipe off fresh glue with a wet rag or wait for the glue to skim over, then scrape it off with a knife or chisel.

Although you can often unclamp a glued-up panel in as little as a half an hour, I like to leave boards clamped up at least two or three hours and preferably overnight. If you won't be working the panel right away, lay it across a couple of stickers on a flat bench. Air circulating around it helps maintain a balanced moisture content, minimizing potential warping.

MINIMIZING PANEL WARPAGE

Reversing the growth rings on boards that make up a large panel will result in the panel remaining relatively flat, even if the individual boards cup.

PULL

The recesses are roughed out with a gouge and mallet and then finished with a small veining tool. The carved black walnut pulls are glued into stepped through mortises that maximize the gluing surface area.

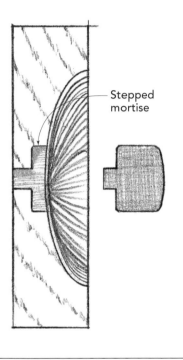

Stepped mortise

Photo L: To make the tenon on the pull, cut two opposing notches in the pull stock, then crosscut the pull free.

of the walnut pull. About ⅜ in. of the pull should project from the bottom of the recess (see "Pull"). The pull should fit snugly enough that you need to seat it with taps from a mallet.

7. Glue the pull into its mortise.

5. Make the T-shaped pulls. First, rip a piece of material ¼ in. thick by 1 in. wide. Then use a ¼-in.-wide dado head to cut two opposing ⅜ in. deep notches, set ½ in. from the end of the piece (see **photo L**). Crosscut the resulting T-shaped section from the piece, then round over the top edges of the pull with sandpaper.

6. Chisel out a stepped mortise at the bottom of the pull recess to accept the bottom section

FINISHING UP

I like the look of natural unstained cherry so I use a Danish oil finish topped off with a coat of wax for a piece like this. However, if your desk is going to sit in a high-traffic area or be subject to a lot of abuse, I would recommend a more durable finish like a solvent-based polyurethane or water-based lacquer.

Greene and Greene Writing Desk

Thomas Stangeland, who designed and built the original version of this desk, is an admirer of the work of Charles and Henry Greene, two California brothers who designed furniture in the early twentieth century. The Greenes were influenced by the work of Gustav Stickly, but they modified the square, bulky look common to the Arts and Crafts movement by incorporating Asian motifs into their designs. On this desk, the delicate, swooping brackets under the aprons, the proud, exposed splines, and the "cloud lift" curves on the breadboard ends, are typical Greene and Greene touches.

Stangeland's desk was originally designed and built as a writing desk, although it could also be used as a side table in a living room or dining room. At first glance, the desktop appears to be a solid-wood panel capped with breadboard ends to help keep it flat. However, the top is actually mahogany plywood, so the breadboard ends are strictly decorative, as are the exposed splines at the breadboard end joints. The side and back aprons appear to be made of frame-and-panel construction, but each apron is actually one solid piece of wood with applied moldings.

The basic desk is relatively simple to make. The challenge lies in the details—making the breadboard end joints, the curved splines and brackets, the drawer pulls, and the decorative pegs. But these elements set this desk apart and are worth the trouble.

Greene and Greene Writing Desk

THE BREADBOARD END CURVES ON THE TOP of this desk are template routed for a matching fit with the top. The splines are strictly decorative. The applied vertical trim pieces and the bottom rails give the aprons the look of frame-and-panel construction.

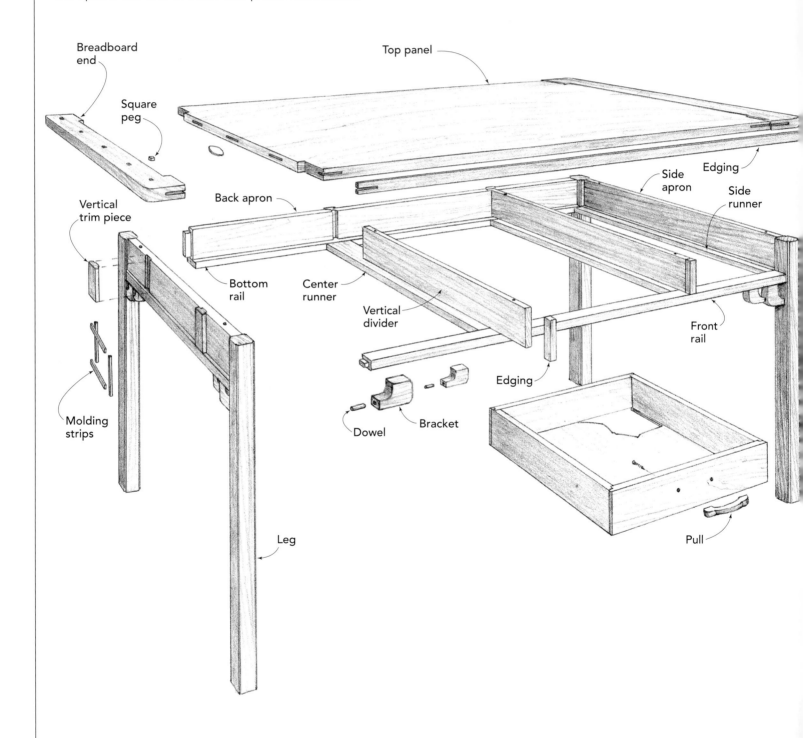

Breadboard end

Square peg

Top panel

Edging

Side apron

Side runner

Vertical trim piece

Back apron

Bottom rail

Center runner

Vertical divider

Front rail

Edging

Molding strips

Dowel

Bracket

Leg

Pull

LEG AND APRON DETAIL

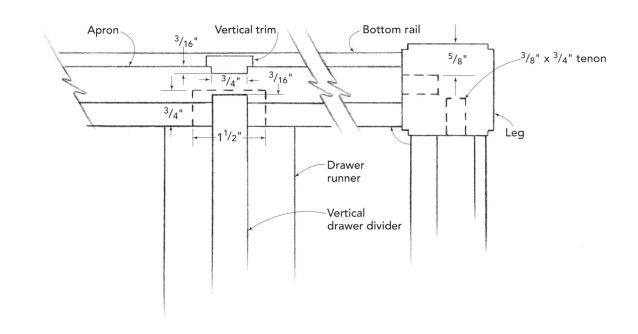

Apron

Vertical trim

Bottom rail

3/16"

5/8"

3/8" x 3/4" tenon

3/4"

3/16"

3/4"

Leg

1 1/2"

Spline

Drawer runner

Vertical drawer divider

FRONT VIEW DETAIL

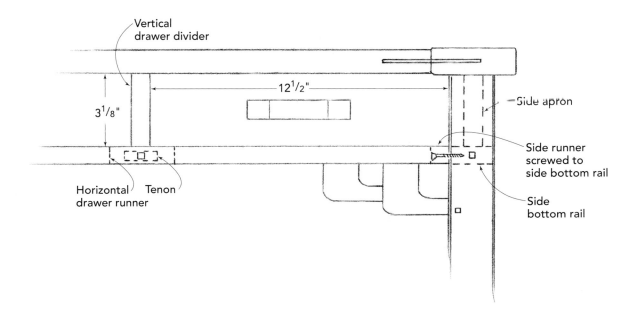

Vertical drawer divider

12 1/2"

Side apron

3 1/8"

Side runner screwed to side bottom rail

Horizontal drawer runner

Tenon

Side bottom rail

TOP VIEW

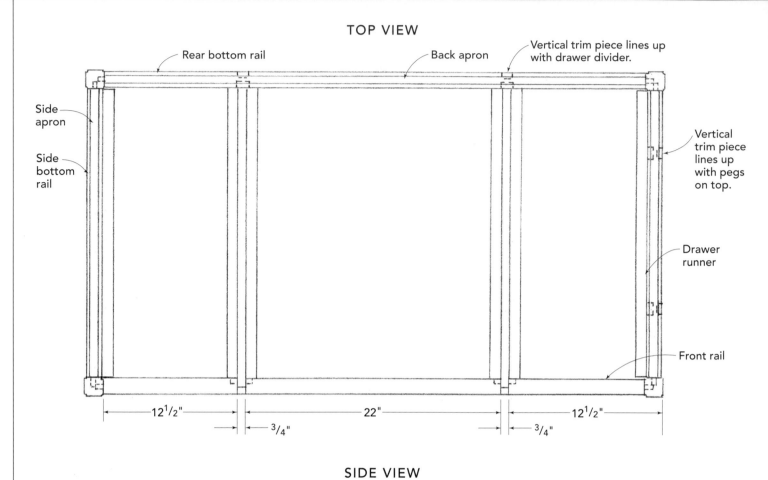

Rear bottom rail

Back apron

Vertical trim piece lines up with drawer divider.

Side apron

Side bottom rail

Vertical trim piece lines up with pegs on top.

Drawer runner

Front rail

12$^1/_2$"

$^3/_4$"

22"

$^3/_4$"

12$^1/_2$"

SIDE VIEW

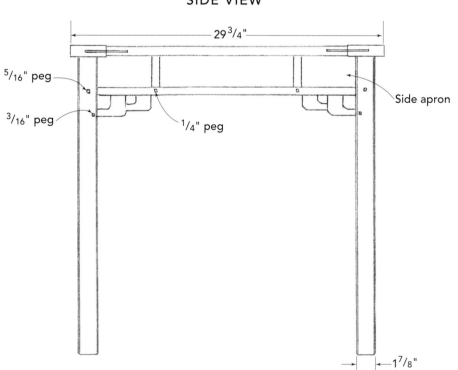

29$^3/_4$"

$^5/_{16}$" peg

$^3/_{16}$" peg

$^1/_4$" peg

Side apron

1$^7/_8$"

FRONT VIEW

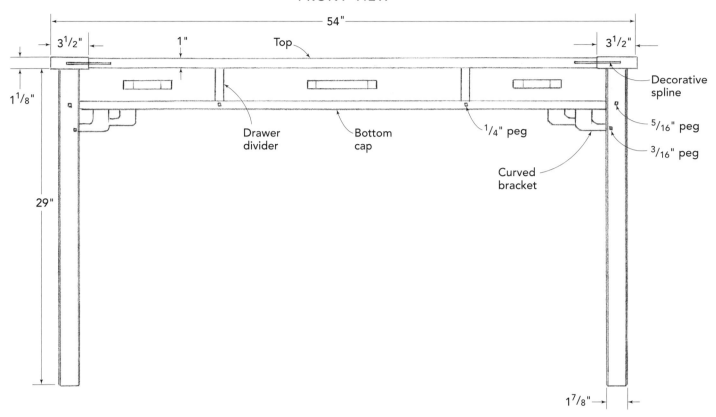

54"

3 1/2"

1"

Top

3 1/2"

Decorative spline

1 1/8"

Drawer divider

Bottom cap

1/4" peg

5/16" peg

3/16" peg

Curved bracket

29"

1 7/8"

BACK VIEW

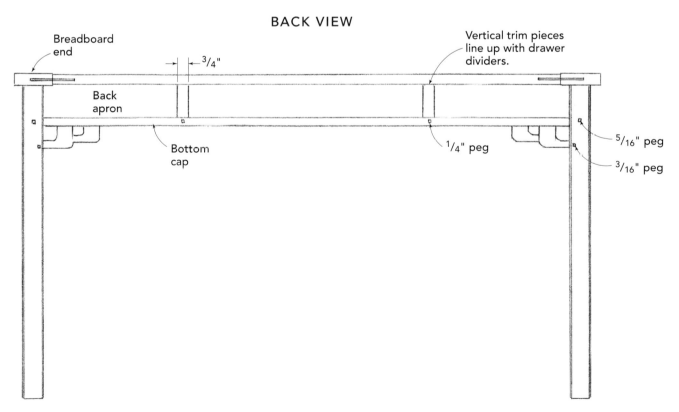

Breadboard end

Vertical trim pieces line up with drawer dividers.

3/4"

Back apron

Bottom cap

1/4" peg

5/16" peg

3/16" peg

BUILDING THE DESK STEP-BY-STEP

CUT LIST FOR GREENE AND GREENE WRITING DESK		
Top		
1	Panel	1 in. x 29⅜ in. x 48 in.
2	Breadboard ends	1⅛ in. x 3½ in. x 29¾ in.
2	Solid-wood edgings	⅛ in. x 1 in. x 48 in.
4	Splines	3/16 in. x ¾ in. x 3½ in.
Base		
4	Legs	1⅞ in. x 1⅞ in. x 29 in.
2	Side aprons	¾ in. x 3⅛ in. x 25⅛ in. (including a ⅜-in. x 2⅝-in. x ¾-in. tenon on both ends)
1	Back apron	¾ in. x 3⅛ in. x 50 in. (including a ⅜-in. x 2⅝-in. x ¾-in. tenon on both ends)
1	Front rail	¾ in. x 1½ in. x 50 in. (including a ⅜-in. x 1-in. x ¾-in. tenon on both ends)
2	Side bottom rails	¾ in. x 1½ in. x 23⅝ in.
1	Rear bottom rail	¾ in. x 1½ in. x 48½ in.
6	Vertical trim pieces	⅜ in. x 1 in. x 3⅛ in.
2	Vertical drawer dividers	¾ in. x 3⅛ in. x 25⅝ in.
2	Drawer divider edgings	¾ in. x ¾ in. x 3⅛ in.
2	Horizontal drawer runners	¾ in. x 2¾ in. x 25½ in. (including a ⅜-in. x 1½-in. x ¾-in. tenon on both ends)
2	Side drawer runners	¾ in. x 1 in. x 23⅝ in.
Outer Drawers		
2	Fronts	¾ in. x 2 15/16 in. x 12½ in.
4	Sides	½ in. x 3 in. x 24 in.
2	Backs	½ in. x 2½ in. x 12 in.
2	Bottoms	¼ in. x 11 15/16 in. x 23¼ in.

CONSTRUCTION OF THE DESK can be broken down into four phases: the top, the base, the drawers, and the fine details. Make the top first, then the base. After making and fitting the drawers, tend to the details, which include making and installing the brackets and the square pegs.

MAKING THE TOP

The top is not a complicated assembly but it does involve making templates for fitting the breadboard ends to the panel.

Creating templates for attaching the breadboard ends

To make the joints for the breadboard ends, you'll need to make a pair of complementary templates for pattern routing the cloud lift profiles on the breadboard ends and the top. Make the templates from a good-quality, void-free, ¼-in.-thick hardwood plywood such as Baltic birch plywood.

1. On your plywood, draw the profile of the breadboard end curve (see "Breadboard End").
2. Saw the shape on the bandsaw, cutting as close to the line as possible while leaving a bit of material to be smoothed with hand tools (see **photo A**).
3. Clean up the edge of the template to the cut line, using a combination of files, rasps, and sandpaper (see **photo B** on p. 78).
4. Use the finished template to lay out the curve on another piece of plywood for making the complementary template.
5. Bandsaw the complementary template as before, sawing a bit shy of the cut line. Then rasp, file, and sand the edges until the two templates match perfectly (see **photo C** on p. 78).

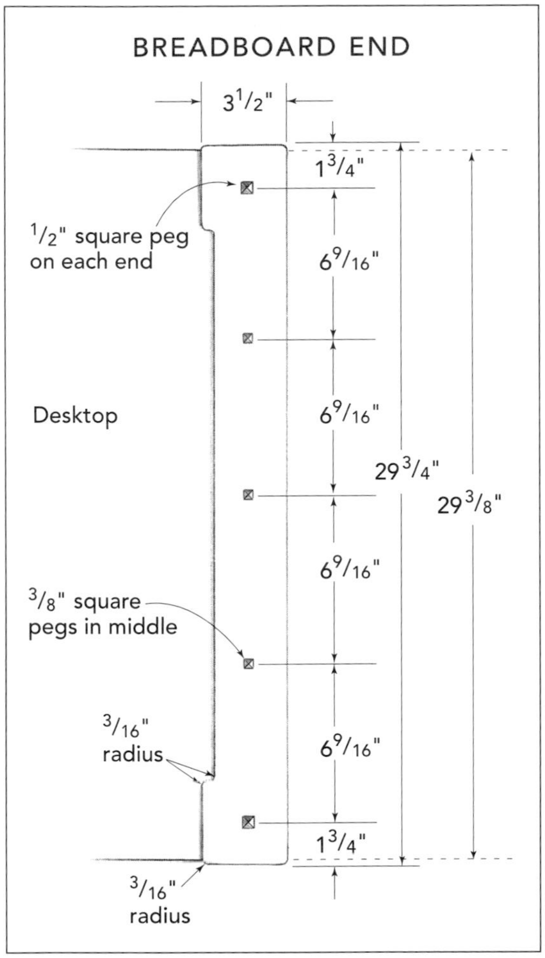
BREADBOARD END
3 1/2"
1 3/4"
1/2" square peg on each end
6 9/16"
Desktop
6 9/16"
29 3/4"
29 3/8"
6 9/16"
3/8" square pegs in middle
3/16" radius
6 9/16"
1 3/4"
3/16" radius

CUT LIST FOR GREENE AND GREENE WRITING DESK

Center Drawer		
1	Front	¾ in. x 2 15/16 in. x 22 in.
2	Sides	½ in. x 3 in. x 24 in.
1	Back	½ in. x 2½ in. x 21½ in.
1	Bottom	¼ in. x 21 7/16 in. x 23¼ in.
Details		
4	Square pegs	½ in. x ½ in. x ⅜ in.
6	Square pegs	⅜ in. x ⅜ in. x ⅜ in.
8	Square pegs	5/16 in. x 5/16 in. x ⅜ in.
8	Square pegs	¼ in. x ¼ in. x ⅜ in.
8	Square pegs	3/16 in. x 3/16 in. x ⅜ in.
8	Bracket blanks	¾ in. x 2⅛ in. x 2¾ in.
8	Bracket blanks	¾ in. x 1 9/16 in. x 2½ in.
2	Drawer pulls	13/16 in. x 15/16 in. x 4⅜ in.
1	Drawer pull	13/16 in. x 15/16 in. x 6½ in.

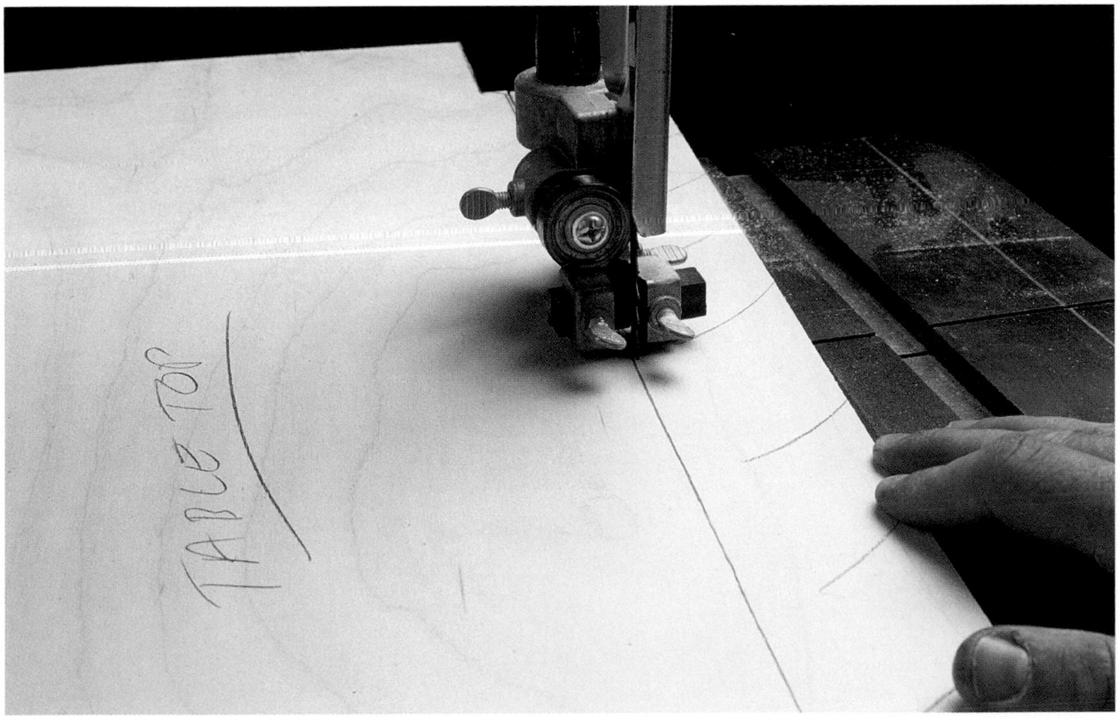
TABLE TOP

Photo A: Saw just shy of the breadboard template cut line, leaving a bit of material to be smoothed with hand tools.

Photo B: Smooth the edge of the template using a combination of files, rasps, and sandpaper.

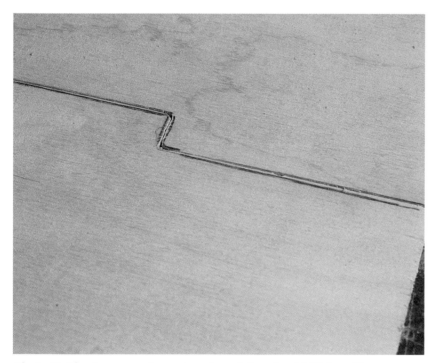

Photo C: The two complementary templates should fit together very snugly.

Shaping the panel

1. Cut the top to size. If you can't find a piece of 1-in.-thick plywood, you can glue and screw together two ½-in.-thick sheets, cutting them slightly oversize initially, then trimming them to length and width afterward.

2. Mill the ⅛-in.-thick by 1-in.-wide edging for the top.

3. Glue the edging to the top, then scrape and sand it flush to the plywood after the glue dries.

4. Using a ¼-in.-radius roundover bit, rout a slight radius on the edges. Adjust the router bit height so the radius starts ⅛ in. down the edge.

5. Use the appropriate template to trace the cloud lift profile onto the underside of the top, then saw the profile with a jigsaw, cutting a bit shy of the line.

6. Screw the template to the underside of the top, realigning it to it to your original pencil line.

7. Rout the profile using a flush-trimming bit guided against the edge of the template.

8. Finish-sand the entire top.

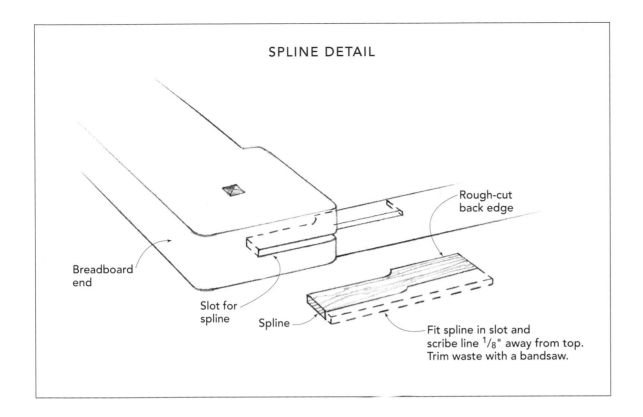

SPLINE DETAIL

Rough-cut back edge

Breadboard end

Slot for spline

Spline

Fit spline in slot and scribe line $1/8$" away from top. Trim waste with a bandsaw.

Making the breadboard ends

1. Dimension the stock for the two bread-board ends.

2. Screw the complementary template to the underside of the breadboard end and repeat the tracing, cutting, and routing procedure as described earlier. Check the fit of the bread-board against the end of the desktop. If your templates are made correctly, the breadboard edges should fit snugly against the ends of the panel.

3. Rout a slight radius on the inside top edge to match the roundover on the edges of the panel.

Attaching the breadboard ends

1. Working from the bottom side of the panel, clamp the breadboard ends to the ends of the panel and mark reference lines across the joint for biscuit slots.

2. Remove the breadboard ends, cut the slots, then lay out and drill the five holes for the square pegs on each breadboard end (see "Breadboard End" on p. 77). Don't bother squaring up the holes right now, you can do that later, chopping all of the desk's peg holes at one time.

3. Glue the breadboard ends to the top.

Making and fitting the splines

1. Rout the ⅛-in.-deep mortises for the exposed splines (see "Spline Detail"). I used a bearing-guided slot-cutting bit (see **photo D** on p. 80). Ride your router on the underside of the table so it's sliding on a flat surface.

2. Chisel the inside corners of each mortise square.

3. Rip the splines to width and cut them to length, then bandsaw the inside curve of each to match the contour of the mortise.

Photo D: A slot-cutting bit is a quick way to rout the mortises for the exposed splines.

3. Slightly ease both edges of each rabbet with a ⅛-in.-radius roundover bit. The cutting edge should remove just enough material to give the rabbet a soft edge (see **photo E**). Touch up the rounded edge with some sandpaper.
4. Cut the legs to length.
5. Cut the mortises for the side and back aprons, setting the mortises back ⅜ in. from the outer faces of the legs. Also cut the mortises for the front rail, which will be stepped back from the face of the leg by ³⁄₁₆ in. (see "Leg and Apron Detail" on p. 73).

Making the aprons

1. Dimension the stock for the aprons and the front rail, remembering to include the length for the tenons.
2. Cut the ³⁄₁₆-in.-deep by ¾-in.-wide dadoes on the outside faces of the aprons that house the vertical trim pieces (see "Top View" on p. 74 and "Front View" on p. 75).
3. Cut the two ³⁄₁₆-in.-deep by ¾-in.-wide dadoes on the inside face of the back apron; these dadoes house the back ends of the drawer dividers. The dadoes line up with the grooves for the vertical trim pieces on the outside of the apron.
4. Cut the tenons on the aprons and front rail, making sure they fit snugly in their mortises.
5. Rip and plane the stock for the bottom rails. Make the pieces oversize in length.
6. Dry-clamp the legs tightly to the aprons, then cut the bottom rails to fit between the legs. The rails should fit tightly enough that you need to tap them in place with a mallet, but not so tight that they force the legs apart.
7. Rip long stock for the vertical trim pieces, sawing the tongue to fit snugly in the apron dadoes. Then crosscut the individual pieces to fit.

4. Fit the splines in their slots and scribe a line ⅛-in. proud of the edge of the top.
5. Bandsaw close to the line, then smooth up to it using files and sandpaper. Remove any saw marks, round the edges, and polish the outer faces. This will be difficult to do once the splines are glued in place.
6. Glue the splines into their mortises, then do any necessary touch-up sanding.

MAKING THE BASE

The 1⅞-in.-square legs are solid and sturdy, but the slightly relieved profile on all four edges keeps them from looking blocky. The aprons are capped on their lower edges with a bottom rail. The rail and the applied vertical trim pieces are what gives the apron assemblies the look of frame-and-panel construction.

Shaping the legs

1. Rip the legs to width, then square them using a jointer, planer, or handplane.
2. Rout a ⅛-in. by ⅛-in. rabbet on each edge of the leg. You could saw the rabbet, but a router bit follows any slight curve in the legs, cutting a consistent depth along the entire length.

Making the drawer dividers and runners

The plywood drawer dividers extend from the rear apron to the front rail. The front end of each divider is capped with a piece of solid

wood. Each center drawer runner attaches to the bottom edges of a divider, creating an inverted T that adds strength to the base. Make the runners from a durable hardwood like white oak, hickory, or maple.

1. Cut the runners to length and width.
2. Lay out and cut the mortises for the center drawer runners in the inside edges of the front and rear rails.
3. Cut the tenons on the ends of the center runners.
4. With the runners dry-clamped in place, cut the dividers to fit, then glue and screw them to the runners.
5. Lay out the holes for the square pegs on the legs and bottom rails.
6. Drill the holes, then chop them square with a chisel (see **photo F**). Of course, if you have a hollow-chisel mortiser, you can cut the square holes in one step. While you're at it, square up the peg holes on the breadboard ends.
7. Disassemble the table and finish-sand all of the parts.

Photo F: If you don't have access to a hollow-chisel mortiser, simply bore out the center of the peg holes, then square them up with a sharp chisel.

8. Drill and counterbore long holes through the aprons and drawer dividers for attaching the desktop.

Assembling the base

1. Begin the assembly of the base by gluing the vertical trim pieces into their dadoes, holding them in place with a couple of small screws or nails from the inside of each apron.

2. Assemble the sides of the base by joining each side apron to its front and back leg. Make sure these subassemblies are flat and square under clamp pressure.

3. Glue the drawer runner/divider assemblies to the rear apron and front rail, then glue the side assemblies to the rear apron and front rail. Make sure the base is square under clamp pressure or fitting the drawers will be difficult.

4. Glue the bottom rails to the back and side aprons.

5. Glue and screw the side drawer runners to the inside edges of the bottom rails on each side apron.

6. Stangeland framed the false panels on the aprons with small quarter-round moldings glued in place. He made the molding by run-

ning a ⅛-in.-radius roundover router bit on the edge of a ⅛-in.-thick board and then ripping off a ⅛-in.-thick strip. You could avoid this step by simply rounding over the edges of the bottom rail and vertical trim pieces with sandpaper.

7. Attach the top to the base by running long screws through each of the holes that you drilled in the three aprons and the two drawer dividers.

MAKING THE DRAWERS

I used a locking tongue-and-groove joint at the front of the drawers and a standard rabbet-and-dado joint at the rear. Alternatively, you could join the drawers with half-blind dovetails at the front and through dovetails at the rear.

1. Cut the drawer fronts to size. If possible, make them all from the same board so the grain pattern can flow naturally from one drawer front to the next.

MAKING A LOCKING TONGUE-AND-GROOVE DRAWER JOINT

A locking tongue-and-groove joint provides relatively good strength for a drawer joint and hides the ends of the drawer sides. The joint can be made in three passes over a ¼-in.-wide dado head on a table saw. The following instructions are for drawers with a ¾-in.-thick front and ½-in.-thick sides.

1. Set your dado head for a ½-in.-deep cut and run the drawer front on end so the dado cut is centered on the end of the piece.

2. Clamp a ¼-in.-thick piece of scrap wood onto the rip fence and adjust the fence so that

the scrap wood is just touching the blade. Lower the dado head for a ¼-in.-deep cut, then cut the dado in the rear face of the drawer front.

3. Remove the scrap wood and cut the dado on the inside face of the drawer side. If your setup was accurate, you should now have a snug-fitting joint.

4. Without changing the last setup, cut a ¼-in.-wide by ¼-in.-deep groove in the bottom inside edges of the sides and drawer front to create the drawer bottom groove.

2. Dimension the drawer sides and back to size. Note that the sides are 1/16 in. wider than the fronts.

3. Cut the locking tongue-and-groove joints for the drawer front corners (see "Locking Tongue-and-Groove Joint").

4. Cut the rabbet-and-dado joints for the rear corners (see **photo G**).

5. Assemble the drawers, aligning the top edges of the drawer front with the top edges of the sides. The resulting 1/16-in. projection at the bottom helps maintain the gap at the bottom of the drawer front and rail.

6. Fit the drawers into their openings, planing or sanding as necessary to create a consistent gap all around the drawer front.

7. Finish-sand the drawers, easing all sharp edges.

Making the drawer pulls

1. Dimension the blanks for the drawer pulls.

2. Trace the shape of each pull on its blank (see "Drawer Pulls" on p. 84).

3. Cut the pulls to shape on a bandsaw, staying a bit outside of the lines.

4. Use a drum sander to clean up the inside curves; a belt sander for the outside curves;

Tip: If a drawer pull is slightly off, enlarge the front end of one of the holes using a bigger drill bit, then adjust the pull and retighten the screw.

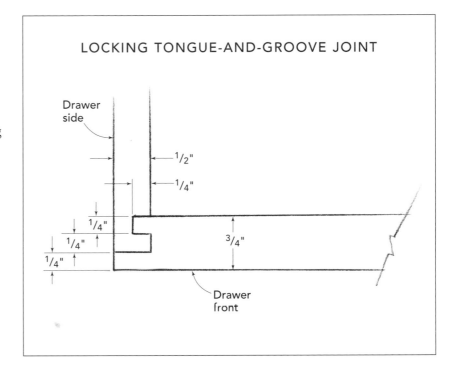

LOCKING TONGUE-AND-GROOVE JOINT

Drawer side

1/2"

1/4"

1/4"

1/4"

1/4"

3/4"

Drawer front

Photo G: I use a rabbet-and-dado joint to connect the drawer sides to the back.

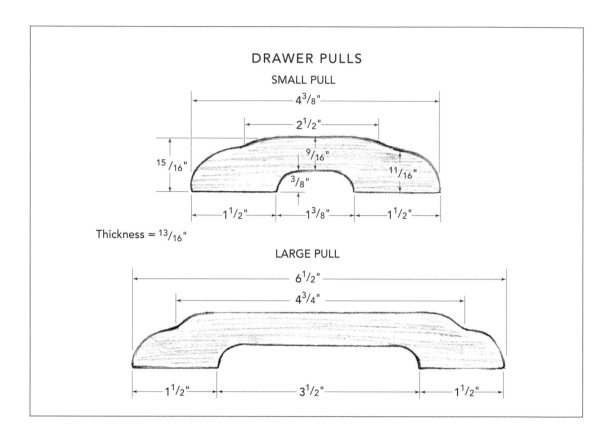

DRAWER PULLS

SMALL PULL

Thickness = $^{13}/_{16}$"

LARGE PULL

and a combination of files, rasps, and sandpaper for the cloud lift steps. Ease all the edges with a file and sandpaper.

5. Install the drawer pulls. Drill two holes through each drawer front, then position the pull over the hole. Slide a nail through each hole and tap it to mark the position of the screw hole on the back of the pull. Drill the holes in each pull, then attach it to the drawer front with a couple of screws.

THE DETAILS

All that's left to the construction is to make and install the 16 curved brackets and the square pegs. Each pair of brackets are doweled to each other and then to a leg. The top edges of the brackets are simply face-glued to the bottom rail.

Making the brackets

1. Cut the bracket blanks to size. It's wise to make a couple of extra blanks of each size in case you make a mistake.

2. Make two stiff cardboard patterns of the brackets (see "Brackets").

3. Trace the shape of the pattern on each bracket.

4. Drill a $^5/_{16}$-in.-diameter by ¾-in.-deep dowel hole centered in the tail end of each bracket.

5. Use a bandsaw to cut the profile of each bracket, cutting a bit shy of your line.

6. Sand to the lines. I sanded the outside diameter on a stationary belt sander and the inside diameter on a drum sander (see **photo H**).

7. Using a belt sander, taper the tail on each small bracket to ⅜ in. thick.

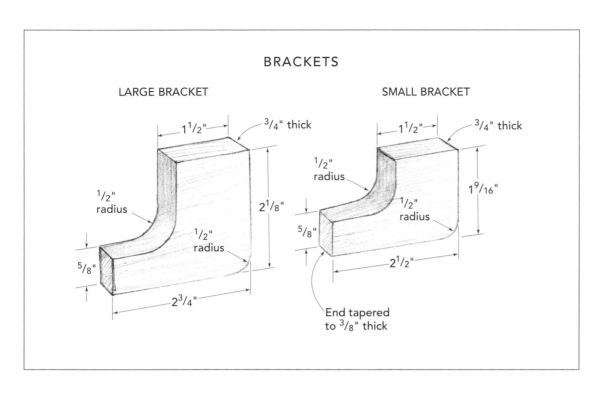

BRACKETS

LARGE BRACKET

$1\frac{1}{2}$"
$\frac{3}{4}$" thick
$\frac{1}{2}$" radius
$\frac{1}{2}$" radius
$2\frac{1}{8}$"
$\frac{5}{8}$"
$2\frac{3}{4}$"

SMALL BRACKET

$1\frac{1}{2}$"
$\frac{3}{4}$" thick
$\frac{1}{2}$" radius
$\frac{1}{2}$" radius
$1\frac{9}{16}$"
$\frac{5}{8}$"
$2\frac{1}{2}$"
End tapered to $\frac{3}{8}$" thick

Photo H: An oscillating spindle sander is ideal for shaping inside curves, but a drum sander chucked in a drill press would also work.

Photo I: The square pegs line up with the intersections of the desk's corner elements. The exposed ends of the pegs are slightly chamfered before insertion and stand about 1/16 in. proud of the adjacent surface.

8. Round over all of the edges except those at the end of each tail. The top edges that meet the bottom rail are only rounded over slightly (see **photo I**). I rounded the edges with a file and some sandpaper, because routing these little pieces would be risky.

Attaching the brackets

1. Pair up the brackets and mark them for their particular locations.

2. Insert a dowel center into the tail end of a small bracket, then lay the pair of brackets upside down on a flat surface. Press the dowel center against the larger bracket to mark the location of the mating dowel hole.

3. Drill the hole in the large bracket, being sure to keep the drill square to the joint face.

4. Keeping the top edges of the brackets aligned on the flat surface, glue the dowel in place, holding the pieces together for a minute or so. Repeat for all bracket pairs and let the glue dry thoroughly.

Photo J: Place the bracket assembly against the bottom rail with a dowel center in the tail hole. (The dowel center shown here actually slips over the dowel itself.) Then press the assembly against the leg to locate the mating dowel hole.

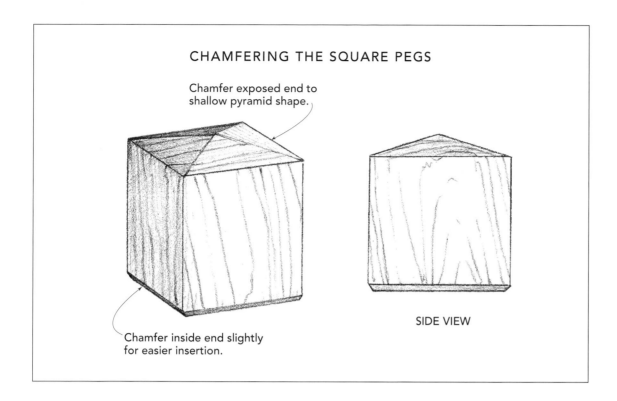

CHAMFERING THE SQUARE PEGS

Chamfer exposed end to shallow pyramid shape.

Chamfer inside end slightly for easier insertion.

SIDE VIEW

5. Insert a dowel center in the tail of the large bracket and place the pair of brackets against the bottom rail. Then press the dowel center into the leg to locate the mating hole (see **photo J**).

6. Drill the hole in the leg, insert the dowel, and glue and clamp the bracket assembly in place.

7. Repeat the above procedures at each corner of the table.

Making and installing the square pegs

1. Dimension short lengths of stock for making the various thicknesses of pegs.

2. Sand four very slight chamfers on both ends of each length of stock to create a very shallow pyramid shape (see "Chamfering the Square Pegs").

3. Cut the length of a peg off the end of each strip.

4. Repeat steps 2 and 3 until you have enough pegs for all of the holes.

5. Slightly chamfer the edges of the opposite end of each peg for easier insertion into its hole. I hold the peg with a pliers and sand the chamfer on a belt or spindle sander.

6. Glue the pegs in place, tapping each one in with a rubber mallet until it's about 1/16 in. proud of the surface.

FINISHING UP

For my money, mahogany is one of the nicest woods to finish. It seems that no matter what you do to it, it always looks good. Because my desk wasn't likely to get much abuse, I simply applied several coats of oil, followed by a coat of wax. I think that the resulting open-grained look is appropriate for this style of furniture. However, if the desk were likely to be subjected to heavy abuse, I would have used a pore filler on the open grain and finished the top with several coats of a hard urethane varnish.

FALL-FRONT DESK

Terry Moore, a furniture maker from Newport, New Hampshire, has built several versions of this contemporary fall-front desk.

It's the proportions and details that make this desk both elegant and highly functional. The tapered legs splay outward slightly in two directions, giving the base a graceful, but sure-footed stance. The rosewood veneers on the front panel and drawers, along with the solid rosewood pulls, complement the mahogany nicely and provide added visual interest. The pigeonhole insert, with all of its compartments, provides ample room for storing notes, papers, and envelopes. The only concession I've made to Moore's design here is to replace the original frame-and-panel case back with a piece of plywood.

This desk is fairly challenging to make and can be a good test of your woodworking skills. The upper case corners are joined with half-blind dovetails, although the rest of the case is simply joined with glue and biscuits. The fall-front assembly—which consists of the fall-flap door and a fall-flap support panel that sits inside the case—incorporates a somewhat tricky joint. The legs attach to the base rails with a mitered, loose tenon joint, which calls for careful layout. And the stretchers attach with a wedged through tenon. However, if you break the desk into its basic components and take one step at a time, it won't be overwhelming to build.

Case

THE CASE IS ASSEMBLED WITH BISCUITS, except for the half-blind dovetails at the top corners. The lower section of the case houses the drawers and lopers. The partition frame is basically a platform for the fall-flap support. The plywood back slides into grooves in the case top and sides after the rest of the case is assembled.

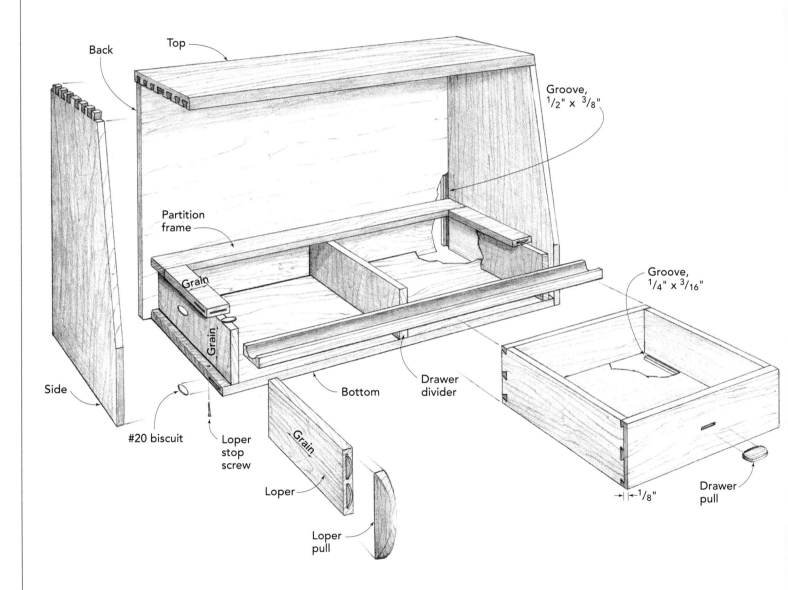

Back

Top

Groove, $1/2"$ x $3/8"$

Partition frame

Grain

Groove, $1/4"$ x $3/16"$

Grain

Side

#20 biscuit

Loper stop screw

Bottom

Drawer divider

$1/8"$

Drawer pull

Grain

Loper

Loper pull

CASE FRONT VIEW

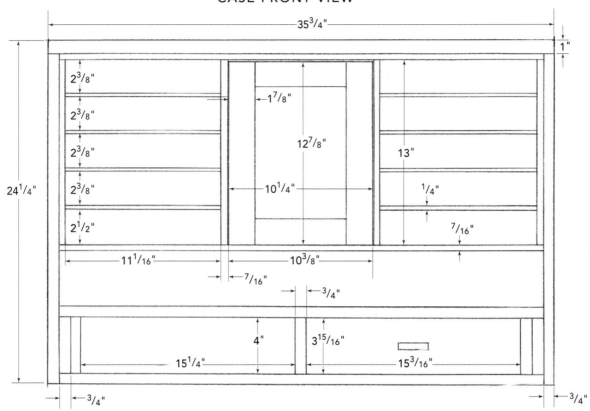

CASE SIDE VIEW

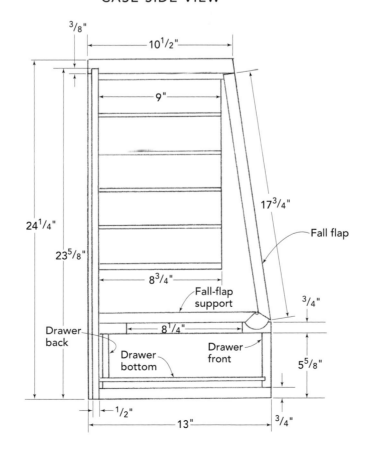

91

Base

THE LEGS ARE VERY SLIGHTLY SPLAYED outward and are joined to the rails with loose tenons. The double-angled joints are cut into the legs first, then traced onto the ends of the rails. The side stretchers connect to the legs with dowels, while the center stretcher attaches to the side stretchers with a wedged through tenon.

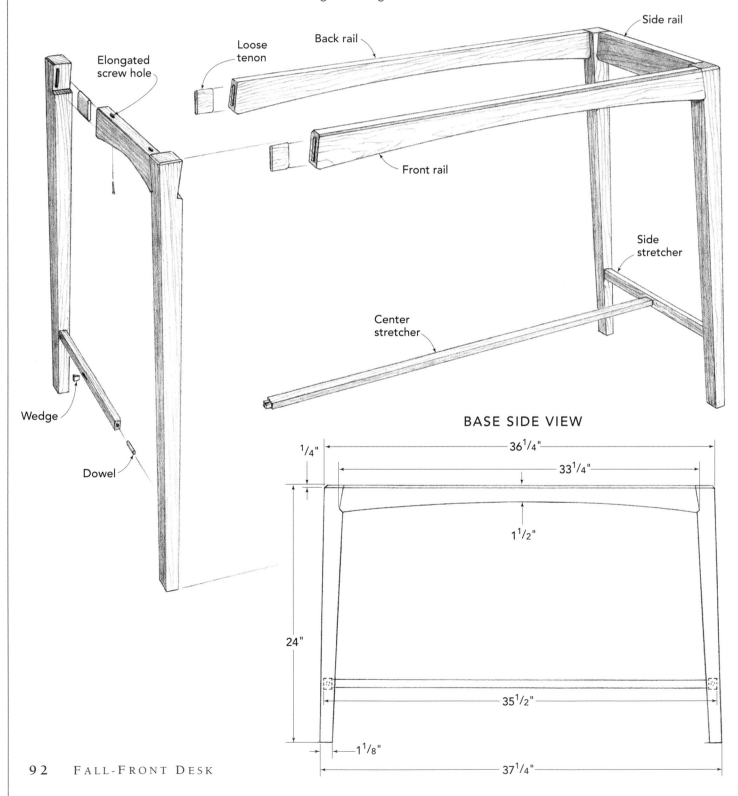

Elongated screw hole

Loose tenon

Back rail

Side rail

Front rail

Side stretcher

Center stretcher

Wedge

Dowel

BASE SIDE VIEW

$1/4$"

$36^1/4$"

$33^1/4$"

$1^1/2$"

24"

$35^1/2$"

$1^1/8$"

$37^1/4$"

BASE SIDE VIEW

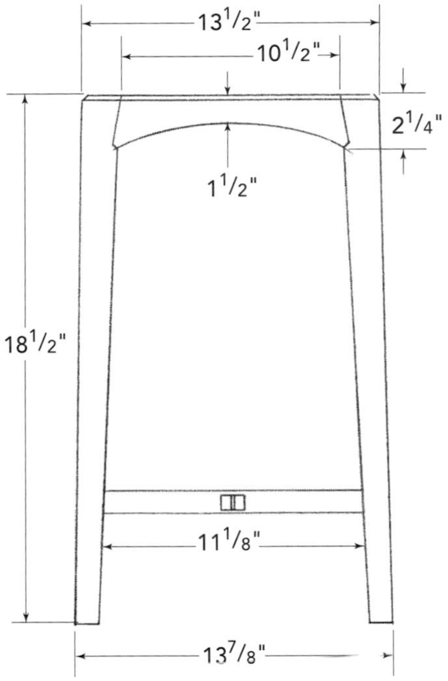

13 1/2"
10 1/2"
2 1/4"
1 1/2"
18 1/2"
11 1/8"
13 7/8"

CUT LIST FOR FALL-FRONT DESK

Base		
4	Legs	1¾ in. x 1¾ in. x 24 in.
2	Side rails	1 1/16 in. x 2¼ in. x 10½ in.
2	Front/back rails	1 1/16 in. x 2¼ in. x 33¼ in.
2	Side stretchers	¾ in. x 1 in. x 11⅛ in. (approximate length)
1	Center stretcher	¾ in. x 1 in. x 35½ in. (approximate length)
Case		
2	Sides	¾ in. x 13 in. x 24 in.
1	Top	1 in. x 10½ in. x 35¾ in.
1	Bottom	¾ in. x 12¼ in. x 34¼ in.
1	Back	½ in. x 23⅝ in. x 35 in.
3	Drawer dividers	¾ in. x 4 in. x 12¼ in.
2	Partition frame front/back rails	¾ in. x 2 in. x 34¼ in.
2	Partition frame end rails	¾ in. x 8¼ in. x 2 in. (cross-grain)
Fall Flap		
2	Stiles	13/16 in. x 2½ in. x 17¾ in. (including a 5/16-in. x 2½-in. x 2½-in. tenon on both ends)
2	Rails	13/16 in. x 2½ in. x 34¼ in.
1	Panel	½ in. x 13½ in. x 30 in. (including a ½-in.-thick x 1-in.-wide solid-wood edging)
1	Fall-flap support	¾ in. x 11⅜ in. x 34¼ in.
8 lin. ft.	Leather tack strips	5/16 in. x ½ in.
Lopers		
2	Lopers	11/16 in. x 3 15/16 in. x 11½ in.
2	Pulls	⅞ in. x 1⅛ in. x 4¼ in.

BUILDING THE DESK STEP-BY-STEP

CUT LIST FOR FALL-FRONT DESK

Drawers		
2	Fronts	5/8 in. x 4 in. x 15 1/4 in.
4	Sides	7/16 in. x 4 in. x 11 7/8 in.
2	Backs	7/16 in. x 4 in. x 15 1/4 in.
2	Bottoms	1/4 in. x 11 7/8 in. x 14 7/8 in.
Pigeonhole Insert		
1	Top	7/16 in. x 9 in. x 34 1/4 in.
1	Bottom	7/16 in. x 8 3/4 in. x 34 1/4 in.
2	Sides	7/16 in. x 8 3/4 in. x 13 in.
2	Dividers	7/16 in. x 8 3/4 in. x 13 in.
8	Fixed shelves	1/4 in. x 8 3/4 in. x 11 9/16 in.
2	Adjustable shelves	1/4 in. x 7 3/4 in. x 10 1/8 in.
Pigeonhole Door		
2	Stiles	3/4 in. x 1 7/8 in. x 13 in.
2	Rails	3/4 in. x 1 7/8 in. x 10 3/8 in. (including a 5/16-in. x 1 7/8-in. x 1 7/8-in. tenon on both ends)
1	Panel	1/2 in. x 7 3/8 in. x 9 5/8 in.
Miscellaneous		
2	Drawer pulls	
1	Door pull	
	Leather	13 in. x 30 in. (approximate size)
8	Adjustable shelf pins	
2	Drop-leaf hinges	1 1/2 in. x 2 7/8 in. (open)
2	Knife hinges	5/8 in.
1	Full-mortise lock	
1	Door catch	

Drop-leaf and knife hinges are available from Woodcraft (see Sources on p. 145).

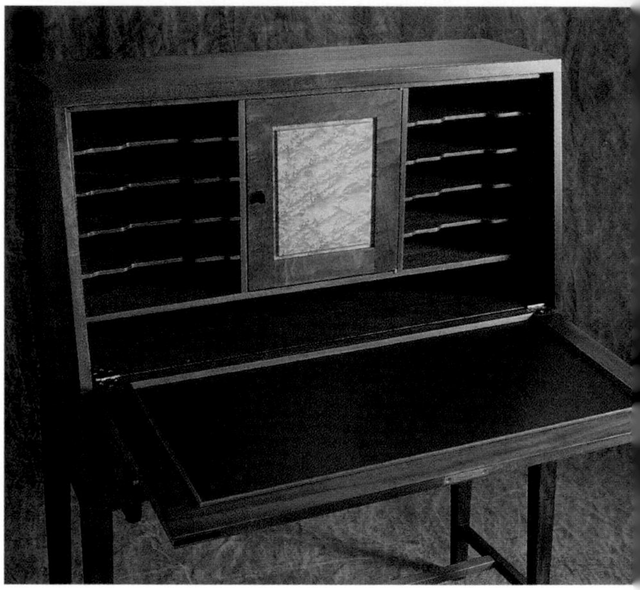

THIS DESK CONSISTS OF five main components: the base, the case, the pigeonhole insert, the drawers, and the fall front. Begin with the base, make the case next, follow that with the drawers and pull-out slides, and finish with the fall front and the pigeonhole insert.

MAKING THE BASE

The base is a bit tricky to make because of the angled leg-to-rail joints and the fact that the leg splay outward slightly. However, if you follow the procedures below and practice making the joints on scrap first, you shouldn't have any major problems. You'll begin by cutting the leg half of each joint, then you'll use those cuts to make a template for laying out the rail half of the joint. After clamping the completed rails to the legs, you'll fit the stretchers directly to the splay of the base assembly.

Making the leg to rail joints

1. Dress the leg blanks to 1¾ in. square. Leave them a bit oversize in length for now. While you're at it, make an extra leg blank to use as a test piece for cutting the joints.

2. Cut the blanks for the rails to thickness, width, and length.

3. Rout the 1¼-in.-deep by 1½-in.-wide leg mortises using a ¼-in.-diameter straight bit (see "Leg Joint").

4. Rout the mating mortises in the squared ends of the rails. Set the mortises back ⅜-in. from the front faces of the rails so they will be flush to the outer faces of the legs (see **photo A**).

5. Mill a strip of ¼-in.-thick by 1⁷⁄₁₆-in.-wide stock for the loose tenons, rounding over its edges afterward to match the ¼-in. radius on the ends of the mortises. Make sure the stock fits snugly into the mortises, but don't cut the individual tenons to length yet.

6. Lay out the leg half of the mitered joint on your test piece (see "Leg Joint"). Then tilt your table saw blade to 45 degrees, and cut the short lower shoulder using your miter gauge to guide the workpiece. Clamp a stop block to the rip fence to index the cut, then saw the short shoulder on all of the legs.

7. Clamp your test piece vertically into a tenoning jig and tilt your saw blade to make the long angled cut (see **photo B** on p. 96). Then make that cut on all of the legs. Alternatively, you could attach a high fence to a miter gauge, clamping the leg to a stop block.

8. Taper the two inside faces of each leg, using a tapering jig on the table saw. The taper should begin just below the bottom edge of the mitered shoulder and diminish to 1⅛ in. square at the foot (see "Base" on p. 92).

9. Make templates for laying out the rail half of each joint. You'll need two templates because the splay of the legs is slightly less on the sides of the desk than at the front and back. To make the templates, begin by tracing the outlines of the front rail and a side rail blank onto a large piece of stiff paper. Position

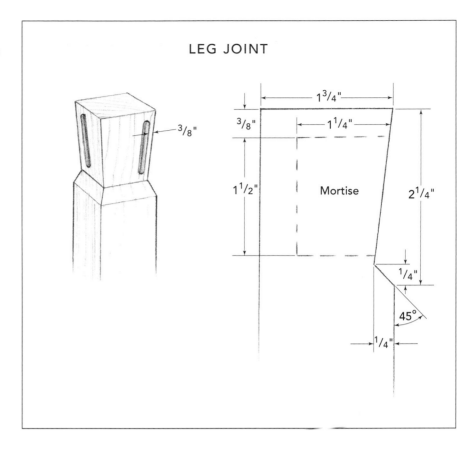

LEG JOINT

Photo A: The lower shoulder on this double-mitered leg joint avoids the weak, short-grain tip common on curved rails.

Photo B: Use a
tenoning jig and a
test piece to set up
the table saw for
cutting the long
angle on the leg
joints.

the legs at the ends of a rail tracing so that the
tip of the V in each leg joint is touching the
end of the rail outline while the top of the leg
is aligned with the top edge of the rail tracing.
Then splay the bottom ends of each pair of
legs outward at the proper distance (see
"Base" on p. 92). Make sure to pivot the leg
around the tip of the V in the leg joint, so that
it remains in contact with the end of the rail
tracing. Then trace the outline of the V onto
the end of each rail tracing to make the layout
templates.

10. Using the templates, lay out the joint on
the end of each rail. Then make the cuts using
a miter saw set to the appropriate angles. This
will guarantee that the ends of each pair of
rails will be cut exactly the same.

11. Cut the spline stock into individual
splines that fit the depth of the joints.

12. Lay out the curve on the bottom of each
rail. To do this, fix each end of a thin ripping
of solid wood to the bottom corner of each
miter shoulder. Flex the strip until it is 1½ in.
away from the top edge of the rail, then trace
along the strip.

13. Cut the curves, then sand them smooth.

Making the stretchers

The side stretchers are attached to the legs
with ⁵⁄₁₆-in.-diameter by 1½-in-long dowels,
whereas the center stretcher is joined to the
side stretchers with wedged through tenons
(see "Base" on p. 92).

1. Dimension the stock for the three stretchers, leaving them well oversize in length.

2. Lay out the angled cuts on the ends of the
side stretchers. To determine the cut lines, lay
the dry-fit leg-and-rail assembly on top of the
stretcher, with the axis of the stretcher located
18½ in. down from the tops of the legs (see
"Base" on p. 92). Trace the inner edges of the
legs onto each stretcher (see **photo C**).

3. Drill a ⁵⁄₁₆-in.-diameter by ¾-in.-deep dowel
hole into the ends of each stretcher, centering
the holes in the stock and drilling parallel to
the axis of the stretcher.

4. Position the stretchers between the legs
and extend lines from the top and bottom
edges of the stretcher across the face of the
leg. Bore a mating dowel hole into each leg,
drilling parallel to the extension lines.

5. Lay out the center stretcher mortise in each of the side stretchers, then cut the mortises.
6. Dry-clamp the base together and mark for the length of the center stretcher by tracing along the outermost edges of the side rails. Then cut the center stretcher to length.
7. Cut the tenons on the ends of the stretcher, then use a handsaw to cut a kerf in the tenon to accommodate a thin wedge (see "Wedged Through Tenon"). Make the wedges in preparation for glue-up.

Assembling the base

1. Dry-fit the base, making sure all of the parts fit together well.
2. While the base is still assembled, use a thin block of wood and a pencil to scribe a cut line parallel to the floor along the bottom end of each leg so the feet will sit flat on the floor.
3. Disassemble the base and trim the bottoms of each leg to the cut line.
4. Glue the side rails and side stretchers to their legs, making sure the assemblies remain flat and symmetrical under clamp pressure.
5. Once the side assemblies are dry, glue them to the front and back rails and center stretcher. Glue the stretcher wedges in place, tapping

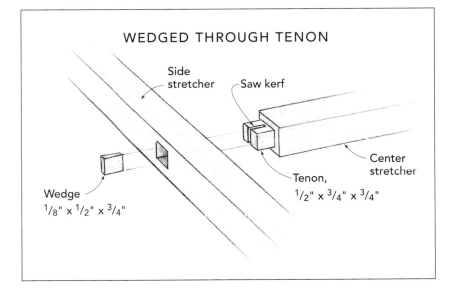

WEDGED THROUGH TENON

Side stretcher

Saw kerf

Center stretcher

Tenon, $1/2$" x $3/4$" x $3/4$"

Wedge $1/8$" x $1/2$" x $3/4$"

them home lightly with a hammer. Let the glue dry thoroughly.
6. Because of the splay of the legs, the top, outside edges of the legs and rails will be slightly canted upward, so plane or sand the entire top edge of the base flat.
7. Rout a 45-degree chamfer all around the upper edge of the base, then finish-sand the entire piece.

MAKING THE CASE

The case is simply a large box that houses the drawers, the fall flap, and the pigeonhole insert. The case and its parts are primarily joined with biscuits, although the top is dovetailed to the sides. Note that the grain on all of the parts, including the partition frame side rails, is oriented in the same direction to prevent cross-grain wood movement problems (see "Case" on p. 90).

Preparing the parts

1. Prepare stock for the sides, top, bottom, drawer dividers, and partition frame. Because the grain on the drawer dividers and the end rails of the partition frame runs across the short dimension of the pieces, it's wise to prepare one board from which to crosscut all of those pieces.

2. Rip and crosscut all of the parts to size. Use a tapering jig on the table saw to cut the angle on the front edge of each case side. Be sure to crosscut the drawer dividers and the partition frame end rails before sawing their short edges square.

3. Saw the bevel on the front edge of the top.

Cutting the case joints

1. Lay out and cut slots for the biscuits that will join the bottom case corners. Also cut the slots for joining the drawer dividers to the case bottom (see "Case" on p. 90).

2. Lay out the half-blind dovetail joints on the top corners of the case (see "Case Dovetails").

3. Cut the half-blind dovetail joints. I cut the tails first, then use them to lay out the pin, but many woodworkers reverse the process.

4. Dry-assemble the case sides to the top and bottom to make sure all of the joints fit well.

Making the partition frame and case back

1. Set up to cut the cove on the front rail of the partition frame (see "Fall-Front Joint"). It's best to lay out the cove on the end of a similarly sized piece of scrap that you can use to set up the cut.

2. To cut the cove, clamp a straight board to your table saw top to serve as a fence. Set the board at an angle to the sawblade and take a light test cut in your scrap piece. Adjust the position of the fence as necessary to center the cove in the workpiece and to cut it to the proper width. Then take a series of light passes until you've reached the full depth of cut (see **photo D**).

3. Assemble the partition frame pieces with biscuits and glue. Make sure the assembly is flat and square under clamp pressure.

4. Stand the drawer dividers in place inside the case, then fit the partition frame snugly inside the case, trimming it as necessary to ensure a tight fit between the case sides. The rear edge of the frame should be ¾ in. from

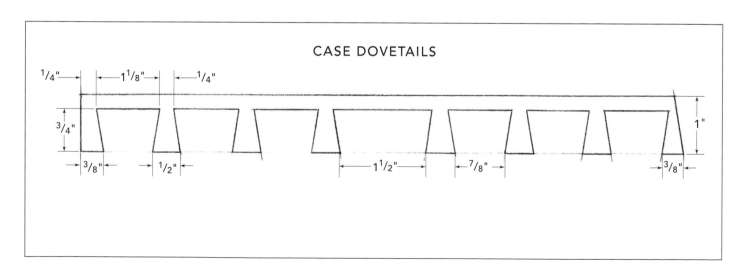

CASE DOVETAILS

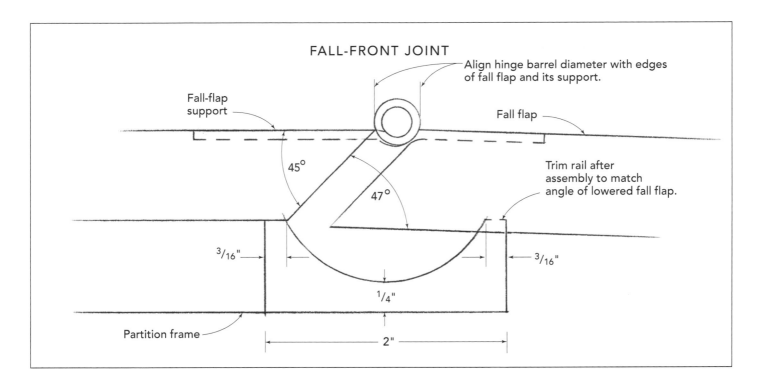

FALL-FRONT JOINT

Align hinge barrel diameter with edges of fall flap and its support.

Fall-flap support

Fall flap

45°

47°

Trim rail after assembly to match angle of lowered fall flap.

3/16"

3/16"

1/4"

Partition frame

2"

the rear case edges to allow passage for the case back.

5. With the case still dry-clamped together, measure for the case back, then cut if from ½-in.-thick hardwood plywood.

Assembling the case

1. Once you're satisfied that all of the case parts fit well, disassemble the case and rout a ½-in.-wide by ⅜-in.-deep groove in the rear edges of the sides and top to accept the case back (see "Case" on p. 90). Make sure to stop the groove ⅜ in. shy of the ends of the top.

2. Finish-sand the interior faces of the case.

3. Glue up the case. Because there are a lot of parts to put together at once, you may want to find a clamping partner and do a dry run to set up your clamps and rehearse your clamping procedures.

4. Glue and clamp the case together, making sure that all of the parts are square and that the width of the drawer openings is correct. Then slide the back into its grooves unglued, fastening it to the rear edge of the case bottom with a few screws.

Photo D: You can cut a cove on the table saw by feeding the workpiece at an angle to the blade, taking a series of light passes.

MAKING THE DRAWERS

The drawers are constructed with half-blind dovetails at the front and through dovetails at the back. The drawer front is made of walnut faced with rosewood veneer. The drawer sides and back are made of solid mahogany.

1. Measure the drawer openings to double-check that they are correct, then cut the drawer fronts, sides, and back to size.

2. Veneer the faces of the drawer fronts by gluing on oversize veneer, then routing it flush to the edges of the drawer front with a flush-trimming bit. (For more on working with veneer, see Book Stand on p. 34.)

3. Lay out the half-blind dovetails for the front corner joints (see "Case" on p. 90). The number and spacing of the tails aren't critical, but make sure that the drawer bottom groove will run through a tail, not a pin.

4. Cut the half-blind dovetail joints. Again, I cut the tails first and then use them to lay out the pins.

5. Lay out and cut the through dovetails for the rear corner joints. The joint spans only the distance from the top edge of the back to the top edge of the drawer bottom groove (see "Case"). (For more on cutting dovetails, see Lap Desk on p. 20.)

6. Saw the ¼-in.-wide by ³⁄₁₆-in.-deep drawer groove into the sides and drawer front of each drawer. The groove is set ½ in. up from the bottom edge of the drawer.

7. Dry-fit the drawer parts to check for good joint fits, then measure for the plywood drawer bottom. It should fit tightly between the side grooves and project a bit more than ¼ in. from the rear of the drawer. The projection, which serves as a drawer stop, will be trimmed when you fit each assembled drawer into its opening.

8. Glue up the drawers, making sure that each one is flat and square when assembled. Sliding the bottom into its grooves will help square things up. After the glue has dried, screw the drawer bottom to the drawer back.

9. Sand the dovetail joints flush, then fit each drawer to its opening. Plane the edges to create a ¹⁄₃₂-in. gap all around the drawer front. Plane the back edge of the drawer bottom

until the drawer front is flush to the front edges of the case.

10. Rout a ³⁄₈-in.-deep by ¼-in.-wide by 1⅜-in.-long mortise into the center of each drawer front to accept the tenon on each pull.

11. Ease any sharp edges with fine sandpaper and lightly sand the drawer front, being careful not to cut through the veneer.

MAKING THE LOPERS

The pull-out slides, called *lopers,* prevent the fall flap from dropping too far and straining or tearing out the hinges. A curved rosewood cap on the front of each loper serves as a pull (see **photo E**).

Photo E: The rosewood loper cap serves as a pull and supports the open fall flap.

1. Mill ¹¹⁄₁₆-in.-thick stock for the lopers, then rip and crosscut it to length to make the two lopers.

2. Rout a ¼-in.-wide by ⅜-in.-deep groove in the bottom edge of each loper, stopping the groove about ½ in. from end of each piece. After the loper is installed, a screw driven up through the case bottom into the groove will prevent the loper from being pulled all of the way out (see "Loper Detail").

3. Make the blanks for the rosewood caps, then cut biscuit slots to attach them to the lopers with two biscuits each.

4. Cut the profile of each cap with a bandsaw, then use files and rasps to complete the shape.

5. Glue the caps to the lopers and sand the assemblies smooth. Check the fit of each loper to make sure it slides freely in the case.

MAKING THE FALL FRONT

The fall-flap half of the fall front is basically a typical frame-and-panel assembly. The panel is made of ½-in.-thick medium-density fiberboard (MDF) edged with solid wood and veneered on the faces with rosewood. The solid-wood edging allows you to rout a profile on the panel's edges, giving it the look of a raised panel. The inside face of the panel, which serves as the desk's writing surface, is covered with leather. The fall flap is attached with drop-leaf hinges to a fall-flap support—a board that rests inside the case on the partition frame (see "Fall Front" on p. 102).

Constructing the frame-and-panel assembly

1. Thickness the stock for the frame stiles and rails and for the fall-flap support. If you don't have a wide enough board for the fall-flap support, edge join boards to create the width.

2. Cut the stiles, rails, and fall-flap support to width and length.

3. Rout the ⁵⁄₁₆-in.-wide by ⅜-in.-deep panel grooves, centering them across the thickness of the rails and stiles. Stop the stile grooves 2 in. from the ends of the stiles.

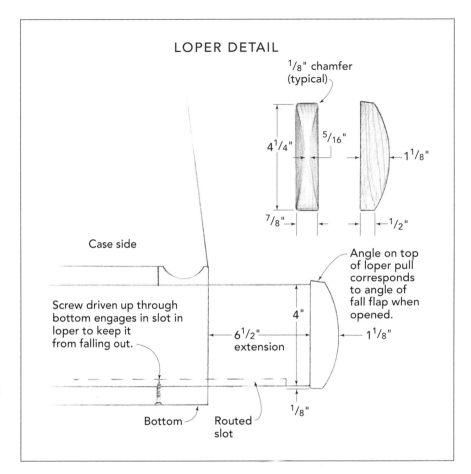

LOPER DETAIL

⅛" chamfer (typical)

4¼"

5/16"

1⅛"

⅞"

½"

Case side

Screw driven up through bottom engages in slot in loper to keep it from falling out.

Angle on top of loper pull corresponds to angle of fall flap when opened.

4"

6½" extension

1⅛"

⅛"

Bottom

Routed slot

4. Set up a dado head on the table saw for a ⁵⁄₁₆-in.-wide cut. Then use a tenoning jig to saw the open mortises on the ends of the rails. Center the cuts across the thickness of the stock. Finish the frame joinery by sawing the mating tenons on the stiles.

5. Cut the MDF panel, then make and apply ¹⁷⁄₃₂-in.-thick by 1-in.-wide solid-wood edging to the panel, mitering it at the corners (see "Fall Front" on p. 102). After the glue dries, scrape the edging flush to the panel (see **photo F** on p. 102).

6. Glue veneer to the front of the panel, leaving its edges just shy of the panel's perimeter.

7. Cut the coved profile on the edges of the panel. I saw away most of the waste on the table saw first, then rout the cove on the router table using a corebox bit (see "Coving the Fall-Flap Panel" on p. 103). The edge of the profile should slip snugly into the panel grooves (see "Fall Flap, Section View" on p. 103).

Fall Front

THE FALL FRONT consists of the frame-and-panel fall flap and the fall-flap support, which tucks inside the case. The two are connected with drop-leaf hinges. The MDF fall-flap panel—which is edged with solid wood and then covered with veneer—is glued into grooves in its frame.

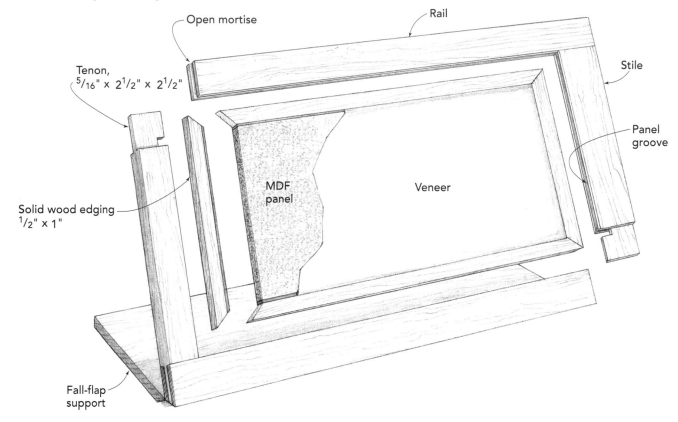

Open mortise

Rail

Tenon, $5/16$" x $2^1/2$" x $2^1/2$"

Stile

Panel groove

Solid wood edging $1/2$" x 1"

MDF panel

Veneer

Fall-flap support

Photo F: A scraper does a good job of leveling the fall-flap panel edging.

8. Carefully scrape and sand the veneer flat and smooth.

9. Cut the 47-degree bevel on the edge of the bottom rail (see "Fall-Front Joint" on p. 99). Because most table saw blades won't tilt far enough to make the cut, first saw the angle to 45 degrees, then increase it to 47 degrees using a handplane.

10. Glue up the frame-and-panel assembly, gluing the panel into its grooves. After the glue dries, scrape and sand the frame joints smooth and flat.

11. Glue the leather to the inside face of the panel (see "Fall Flap, Section View"). Use yellow or white glue, but not so much that it

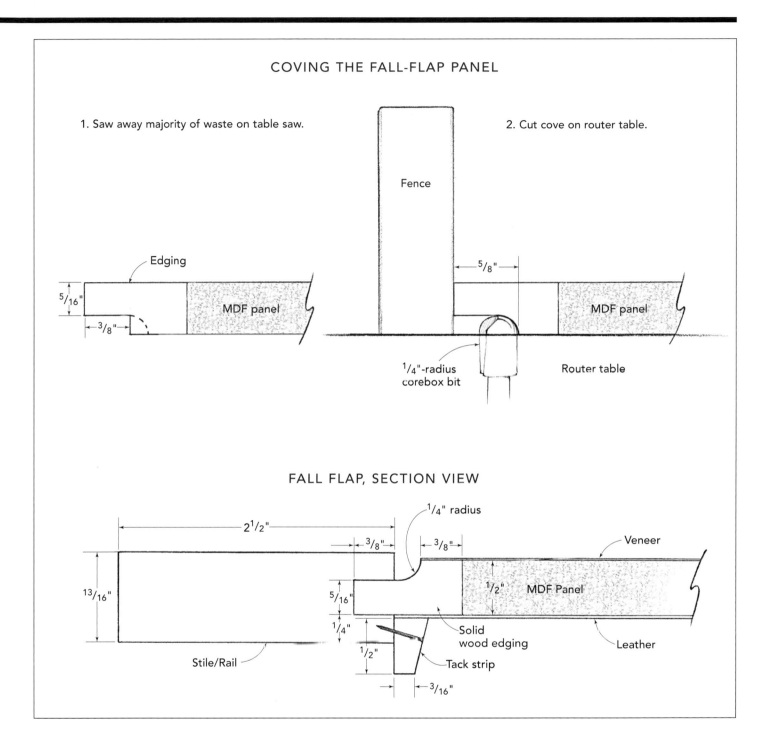

COVING THE FALL-FLAP PANEL

1. Saw away majority of waste on table saw.

2. Cut cove on router table.

Fence

Edging

$5/16$"

$3/8$"

MDF panel

$5/8$"

MDF panel

$1/4$"-radius corebox bit

Router table

FALL FLAP, SECTION VIEW

$1/4$" radius

$2^1/2$"

$3/8$"

$3/8$"

Veneer

$13/16$"

$5/16$"

$1/2$"

MDF Panel

$1/4$"

$1/2$"

Stile/Rail

Solid wood edging

Tack strip

Leather

$3/16$"

might bleed through the leather. Clamp a large caul over the leather to hold it in place (see "Leather Writing Surfaces" on p. 104). **12.** Make the tack strips that border the leather panel (see "Fall Flap, Section View"). The strips hide the edges of the leather and

prevent pens from rolling off the writing surface. Fit the strips tightly within the inside edges of the frame, mitering them at the corners. Then sand them and set them aside.

LEATHER WRITING SURFACES

A leather overlay on a desktop or fall flap creates a comfortable but firm writing surface. Applying leather to wood isn't any more difficult than veneering. Begin by choosing a color that will complement the surrounding wood. Leather is available from many craft-supply stores and furniture upholstery shops. You don't need the most expensive leather for a writing surface, but it should be a good-quality, medium grade that's not too soft.

To attach leather to wood, roll a thin coating of yellow or white glue onto either the wood or the leather. But don't apply so much that it seeps through the leather and stains the surface. Lay the leather flat on the wood, then smooth it down from the center outward, using your hand or a cork-backed block of wood. If the leather is stiff, try misting it with water on the back to make it a bit more pliable. Clamp a flat board on top of the leather to help distribute even pressure over the entire surface. If you anticipate glue seepage through the leather, place a piece of waxed paper between it and the clamping board.

After the glue dries, trim any excess leather from the edges with a sharp knife. You don't really need to maintain the leather in any way, but a yearly coat of leather preservative certainly won't hurt.

Installing the fall front

1. Crosscut the fall-flap support so that it fits tightly between the case sides. But leave it oversize front-to back for right now.
2. Rip the 45-degree bevel on the front edge (see "Fall-Front Joint" on p. 99).
3. Lay the fall-flap support and the fall flap next to each other on a benchtop, centering them along their overlapping beveled edges. Place ¹⁄₁₆-in.-thick shims under the ¾-in.-thick fall-flap support to raise it up to the level of the ¹³⁄₁₆-in.-thick fall flap.
4. Lay the drop-leaf hinges across the overlap, with each hinge in line with the center of a fall-flap stile.
5. Adjust the gap between the two pieces so that the outside edges of the hinge barrel line up with the edges of the two pieces (see "Fall-Front Joint" on p. 99). Be sure to place the long half of each hinge on the fall-front support to prevent the hinge screws from popping through the bevel.
6. Trace the outline of each hinge using a sharp knife, then cut out the mortises.
7. Install the hinges into their mortises.
8. To prepare for fitting the fall front, attach a temporary stop to the inside face of the case top. Cut one end of the stop to match the angle on the front of the case, then use double-sided tape to attach the stop ¹³⁄₁₆ in. back from the front edge of the case.
9. Slide the fall-front assembly into the case until the back edge of the support panel touches the case back. If necessary, trim a bit off the edges of the fall flap to allow it to fit between the case sides.
10. Plane the back edge of the fall-flap support until the face of the fall flap is flush to the sides of the case.
11. Plane the top and side edges of the fall flap to create a consistent gap of about ¹⁄₁₆ in. all around it.
12. At this point you'll need to trim the front edge of the partition frame rail to allow the fall flap to drop slightly below horizontal (see "Fall-Front Joint" on p. 99). You can use a block plane to trim most of the rail, but you'll need to switch to a chisel and scraper as you approach the case sides. Gauge your progress by occasionally lowering the fall flap. You're done when it touches the loper pulls, with the lopers extended 6½ in.
13. Install a full-mortise lock into the top edge of the fall flap, then mortise the striker plate into the top of the case.
14. Remove the fall-front assembly from the case, finish-sand it, then set it aside.

MAKING THE PIGEONHOLE INSERT

The pigeonhole insert consists of four vertical panels that fit between a top and a bottom panel. Four fixed shelves are housed in dadoes in the two outermost sections of the pigeonhole case. The center section, which is

PIGEONHOLE INSERT

The insert is constructed by first gluing the fixed shelves into their stopped dadoes, then gluing and screwing the top and bottom to the two side units.

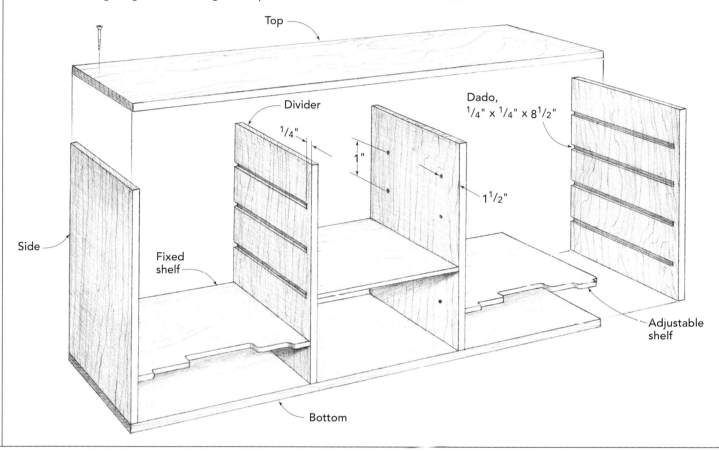

Top

Divider

$1/4"$

$1"$

Dado,
$1/4" \times 1/4" \times 8^{1/2}"$

$1^{1/2}"$

Side

Fixed
shelf

Adjustable
shelf

Bottom

enclosed by a door, houses two adjustable shelves that rest on shelf pins (see "Pigeonhole Insert").

Making the case

1. Dimension all of the parts, cutting them to thickness, width, and length.

2. Lay out the ¼-in. by ¼-in. dadoes for the fixed shelves. Moore spaced the top four shelves 2⅜ in. apart (see "Case Front View" on p. 91).

3. Rout the dadoes, stopping them ¼ in. shy of the front edge of the case.

4. Drill two rows of blind holes in the inside faces of the dividers for the adjustable shelves. Moore spaced the holes 1 in. apart and set the

Photo G: A scrap board with guide holes is handy for drilling holes in case sides for adjustable shelves.

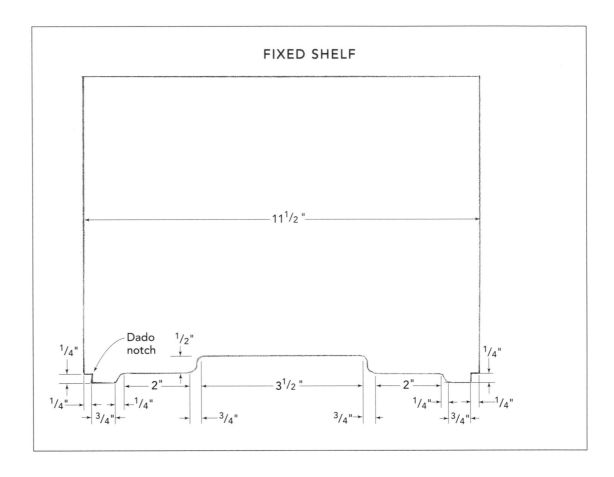

FIXED SHELF

11¹/₂ "

Dado notch

¹/₄ "   ¹/₂ "   2"   3¹/₂ "   2"   ¹/₄ "

¹/₄ "   ¹/₄ "   ¹/₄ "

³/₄ "   ³/₄ "   ³/₄ "   ³/₄ "   ¹/₄ "

rows 1½ in. in from the front and back edges of the case. A shopmade jig for drilling shelf holes makes easy work of this (see **photo G** on p. 105).

5. Cut the profile along the front edge of each fixed shelf (see "Fixed Shelf"). The most efficient way to do this is by first making a template, then using it to cut the profiles with a bearing-guided straight bit.

6. Cut the ¼-in. by ¼-in. notches at the outside corners of each shelf to allow the sides to slip into the stopped dadoes.

7. Finish-sand all of the interior faces in preparation for assembly.

8. Glue and clamp the fixed shelves to the sides and dividers. Spread the glue carefully, because any squeeze-out will be difficult to remove afterward. Make sure the assemblies are square under clamp pressure, then let the glue dry thoroughly.

9. Attach the case top and bottom to the fixed shelf assemblies with glue and screws.

Check to make sure that the entire insert is square and that the back edges of all the pieces are flush.

Making the door

The pigeonhole door is made just like the fall flap, except the door panel is solid bird's-eye maple instead of veneered MDF. Knife hinges attach the door to the case, and a tapered rosewood door pull provides a nice little accent.

1. Dimension the stiles and rails, then cut the frame corner joints and panel grooves in the same manner as you made the fall flap. Just remember that, in addition to narrower rails and stiles, this door is ¹⁄₁₆ in. less in thickness than the fall flap, so you can't use the exact same router table setup to rout the panel grooves.

2. Dry-fit the frame joints, then measure for the panel. Because the panel is solid wood,

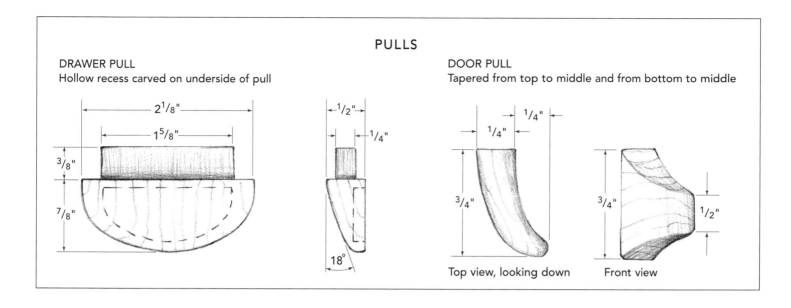

PULLS

DRAWER PULL
Hollow recess carved on underside of pull

2 1/8"
1 5/8"
3/8"
7/8"
1/2"
1/4"
18°

DOOR PULL
Tapered from top to middle and from bottom to middle

1/4"
1/4"
3/4"
3/4"
1/2"

Top view, looking down   Front view

you'll need to allow for wood movement when trimming it to fit the grooves (see "Dealing with Wood Movement," on p. 13).

3. Cut the edge profile using exactly the same techniques and setup as you used for coving the edge of the fall flap.

4. Finish-sand the panel and apply a coat of finish to the sides and edges before gluing up the door. This prevents exposing unfinished edges if the panel shrinks and helps prevent glue from sticking to the panel and locking it in place.

5. Once the finish has dried, glue the door together, making sure that it's flat and square under clamp pressure.

6. Install the knife hinges, then trim the edges of the door to create a consistent gap of about 1/16 in. all around it.

7. Make the door pull and screw it on through the back of the stile. While you're at it, make the drawer pulls (see "Pulls"). Then glue them into the drawer fronts.

8. Remove the hinges, finish-sand the door, and set it aside.

FINISHING UP

1. Apply a finish to all the parts. The numerous compartments and the open-grain mahogany make this an ideal candidate for an oil finish, which is what Moore used. He applied six coats of Danish oil with a little gloss urethane added to it. The first two coats were applied heavily and allowed to dry for several days before being wet sanded. Each of the next four coats was applied thinner and was rubbed with steel wool after it dried.

2. Begin final assembly by attaching the tack strips to the fall-flap frame around the edges of the leather (see "Fall Flap, Section View" on p. 103).

3. Attach the case to the base with screws through counterbored holes in each of the base side rails (see "Base" on p. 92). Use a round file to elongate the holes at the top of the rails to allow the case to expand and contract with seasonal changes.

4. Slide the pigeonhole insert into the case and screw it to the case walls.

5. Insert the lopers, then install a screw through the bottom of the case into each loper groove 4½ in. from the front of the case (see "Case" on p. 90).

6. Insert the hinged fall-front assembly into the case and screw it in place through the partition frame rails.

7. Install the pigeonhole door, place the adjustable shelves on support pins inside the center section, and insert the drawers.

STAND-UP DESK

Jim Becker, a furniture maker from Wilder, Vermont, built this cherry desk for a lawyer who wanted to be able to stand up and stretch his legs now and then while continuing to work. A stand-up desk built along the lines of a tall drafting table seemed to be the ideal solution. Made primarily of 6/4 and 8/4 stock, the desk appears solid and substantial. However, the light, open space around the legs, the curved center stretcher, and the adjustable, tilting top keep the desk from appearing too heavy or massive.

Although this desk was designed specifically for reading and writing, it would also make an ideal platform for drawing or sketching. In fact, the basic design is very versatile and can be altered to suit a variety of needs. For example, you could easily install a drawer below the upper case or you could scale down the dimensions and use the desk as a podium or book stand.

The beauty of this piece lies in its simplicity. It does not have very many parts and is relatively easy to build. It does, however, have a few interesting details that present a bit of a challenge. The top, which can be raised and lowered, is held in place with a ratchet mechanism that pivots on a doweled hinge. And the curved front stretcher is covered with a brass, crescent-shaped scuff plate. Finally, a delicately shaped ledge made of maple keeps pencils and papers from sliding off the desk, while adding an element of visual interest.

Stand-Up Desk

THIS TALL DESK ALLOWS YOU to stand and stretch while working. A ratchet mechanism inside the case supports the top at various angles. The basic "box-on-stand" design incorporates simple mortise-and-tenon and biscuit joinery. The attractive brass scuff plate protects the stretcher while providing a place to rest your feet.

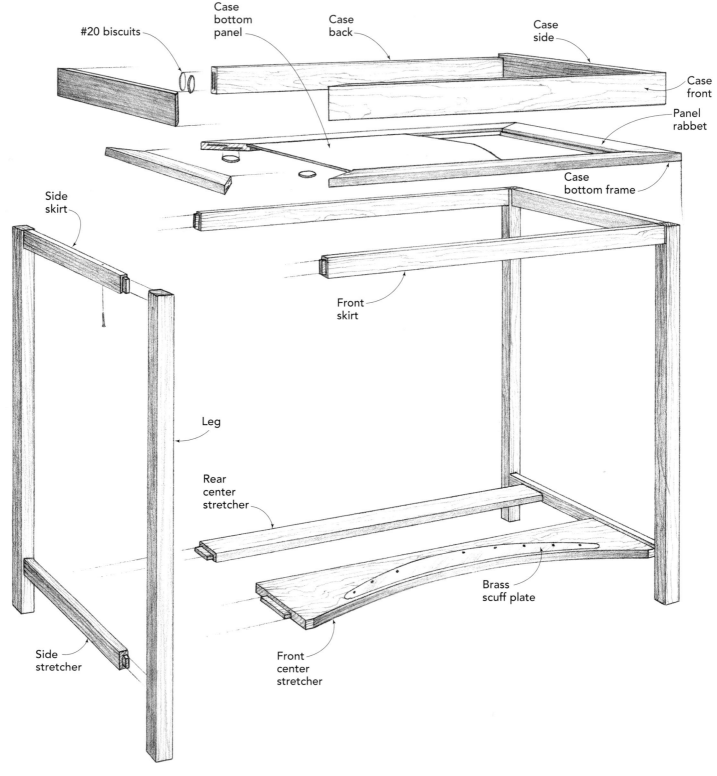

#20 biscuits

Case bottom panel

Case back

Case side

Case front

Panel rabbet

Case bottom frame

Side skirt

Front skirt

Leg

Rear center stretcher

Brass scuff plate

Side stretcher

Front center stretcher

FRONT VIEW

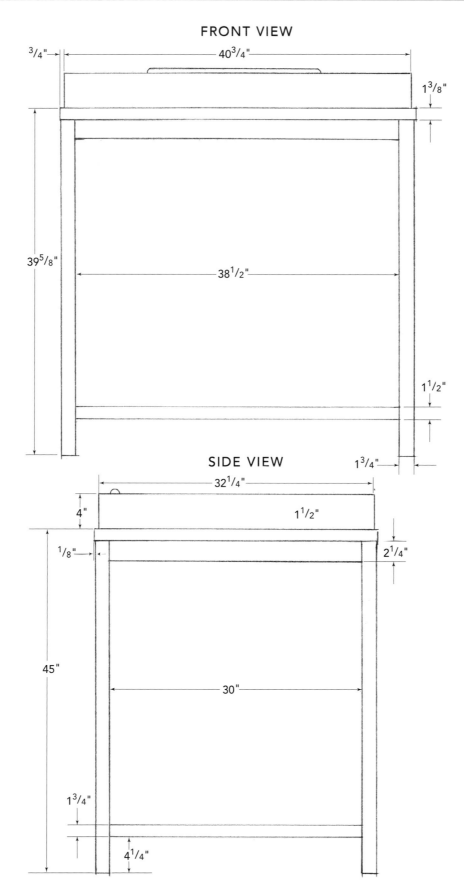

3/4"

40³/₄"

1³/₈"

39⁵/₈"

38¹/₂"

1¹/₂"

1³/₄"

SIDE VIEW

32¹/₄"

4"

1¹/₂"

1/8"

2¹/₄"

45"

30"

1³/₄"

4¹/₄"

BUILDING THE DESK STEP-BY-STEP

THE DESK CONSISTS OF two basic components: a case and its supporting base. The case is really nothing more than a box consisting of a frame-and-panel bottom, four sides, and a lid. The case houses a ratchet mechanism for supporting the top at various angles. The base is made up of four legs, four skirts, and four stretchers.

MAKING THE BASE

Making and mortising the leg

1. Begin by squaring up and dimensioning the legs. It's best to start with 8/4 stock, but if you can't find material this thick, you could glue the stock together from thinner pieces. Just be aware that a glueline and conflicting grain patterns on a leg can disrupt the visual continuity of the desk.

2. Mark the legs for position, then lay out the leg mortises for the skirts and the side stretchers (see "Base Joinery" on p. 114). Each side stretcher mortise should begin 4½ in. from the bottom of the leg.

3. Cut the mortises. You can rout them, cut them with a hollow chisel mortiser, or drill and chop them out by hand.

Making the rails and stretchers

1. Dimension the stock for the rails and stretchers. When crosscutting the pieces to length, remember to allow for the tenons. If you don't have a board wide enough for the front center stretcher, glue two or three pieces together to make up the width. Don't cut the curved profile on the front stretcher yet, because it's much easier to cut tenons on a square piece than on a curved one.

CUT LIST FOR STAND-UP DESK

Base

4	Legs	1¾ in. x 1¾ in. x 39⅝ in.
2	Front/rear skirts	1¹⁄₁₆ in. x 2¼ in. x 40 in. (including a ½-in. x 1¾-in. x ¾-in. tenon on both ends)
2	Side skirts	1¹⁄₁₆ in. x 2¼ in. x 31½ in. (including a ½-in. x 1¾-in. x ¾-in. tenon on both ends)
2	Side stretchers	1½ in. x 1¾ in. x 31½ in. (including a ½-in. x 1¼-in. x ¾-in. tenon on both ends)
1	Rear center stretcher	1½ in. x 3 in. x 40 in. (including a ½-in. x 2½-in. x ¾-in. tenon on both ends)
1	Front center stretcher	1½ in. x 12 in. x 40 in. (including a ½-in. x 8-in. x ¾-in. tenon on both ends)

Case

2	Bottom frame front and rear	1⅜ in. x 3½ in. x 42¼ in.
2	Bottom frame sides	1⅜ in. x 3½ in. x 33¾ in.
1	Bottom panel	½ in. x 27¾ in. x 36¼ in.
1	Case front	1⅜ in. x 4 in. x 40 ¾ in.
1	Case back	1⅜ in. x 3¼ in. x 38 in.
2	Case sides	1⅜ in. x 4 in. x 32¼ in.
1	Top	¾ in. x 31¼ in. x 38¾ in.
1	Ledge	½ in. x ¾ in. x 18¾ in.

Ratchet Mechanism

2	Battens	¾ in. x 3 in. x 25½ in.
1	Hinge dowel	¾ in. diameter x 37½ in.
2	Ratchet bars	¾ in. x 2 in. x 25½ in.
2	Pawls	¾ in. x 2 in. x 6 in.
1	Crossbar	¾ in. x 2 in. x 32¾ in. (including a ⅜-in. x 1-in. x ½-in. tenon on both ends)

Miscellaneous

5	Barrel hinges	14 mm
1	Brass scuff plate	
2	Bullet catches	

Base Joinery

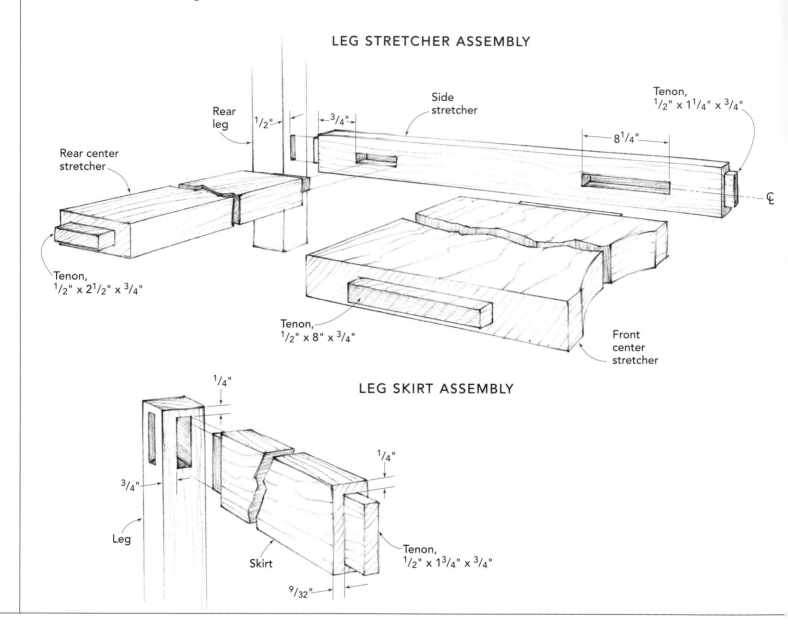

LEG STRETCHER ASSEMBLY

Rear leg

Side stretcher

Rear center stretcher

Tenon, $1/2$" x $1^1/4$" x $3/4$"

$1/2$"

$3/4$"

$8^1/4$"

Tenon, $1/2$" x $2^1/2$" x $3/4$"

Tenon, $1/2$" x 8" x $3/4$"

Front center stretcher

LEG SKIRT ASSEMBLY

$1/4$"

$1/4$"

$3/4$"

Leg

Skirt

Tenon, $1/2$" x $1^3/4$" x $3/4$"

$9/32$"

2. Lay out and cut the center stretcher mortises on the side stretchers (see "Base Joinery"). Because the center front stretcher is so wide, it will expand and contract more than the other parts, so make the mortise about ¼ in. wider than the tenon.

3. Cut all of the tenons on the skirts and stretchers. The tenons should fit snugly into their mortises, requiring only moderate hand pressure to bring the parts together.

4. Lay out the curve on the front center stretcher. The curve exactly matches the curve on the front edge of the brass scuff plate (see "Scuff Plate Pattern").

5. Use a bandsaw or a jigsaw to cut the curve, then smooth the cut with a drum or belt sander.

Assembling the base

1. Dry-fit the entire base assembly to make sure the joints are all tight and that the assembly is square.

2. Disassemble the base and finish-sand the parts. Break all of the sharp edges with sandpaper, but be careful that you don't oversand the pieces and lose the crisp, even lines.

3. Glue up the two side assemblies, joining the side skirts and side stretchers to the legs. Make sure each assembly is flat and square under clamp pressure. Let it dry thoroughly.

4. Remove the clamps and plane or sand the inside faces of the side stretchers flush with the adjacent faces of the legs.

5. Glue the side assemblies to the front and rear skirts and to the center stretchers. When gluing the front center stretcher joints, apply glue to only about the central third of the joint, so the piece can expand and contract without cracking.

6. Check to make sure the assembly is square under clamp pressure and that the side assemblies are not racked in relation to each other. Let the glue dry thoroughly.

MAKING THE CASE

The case consists of three basic components: the top, the bottom, and the wall assembly. Make the top first, so it can be drying while you complete the rest of the case.

Making the case box

1. Begin by laying out the boards for the top. Because the top is the most visible part of the desk, select boards that have good color and interesting figure. Take care to match the grain on adjacent pieces to disguise the glue-lines (see **photo A** on p. 116).

2. Thickness plane and joint the boards, then edge glue them together to make the top. Make it slightly oversize in length and width for right now.

3. Make the bottom frame. Dimension the pieces, miter them at the corners, then glue the frame together with a pair of #20 biscuits at each corner (see "Stand-Up Desk" on p. 110).

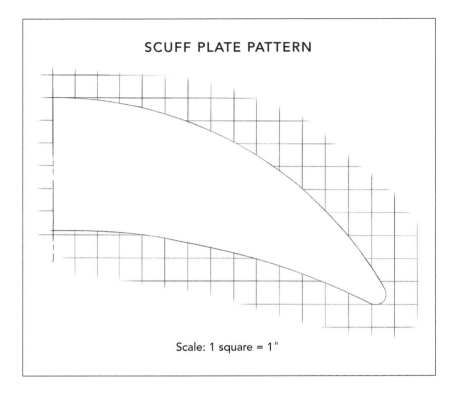

SCUFF PLATE PATTERN

Scale: 1 square = 1"

4. Plane or sand the bottom frame so the joints are all flat and smooth.

5. Rout a ½-in.-wide rabbet into the inner top edge of the frame to accept a plywood panel. It's important that the panel be flush to the frame, so use your panel material to gauge the depth of the rabbet. After routing, square up the rabbet corners with a chisel.

6. Cut a piece of ½-in.-thick hardwood plywood to fit snugly into the rabbet, then glue and tack it into place.

7. Mill the stock for the case sides, front, and back. If possible, cut the stock for the sides and front from the same board. That way, you can glue them together in sequence later, creating an uninterrupted grain pattern around the front of the desk (see **photo B** on p. 116).

8. Miter the ends of the case front and the front ends of the case sides. Then cut a ½-in.-wide by ¾-in.-deep rabbet into the inside top edge of the front and the sides (see **photo C** on p. 117). The rabbet supports the top when it's closed.

9. Cut biscuit slots for the corner joints, then glue the sides, front, and back together. After

Photo A: An attractive panel begins with careful grain and color matching. Notice how the joint between the top two boards virtually disappears, whereas the dissimilar grain orientation and color of the middle and lower boards draws attention to the joint.

the glue dries, plane the top and bottom edges and sand the outside faces of the box.

10. Glue and screw the case bottom to the case walls, making sure the box is square and centered evenly on the frame.

Completing and fitting the top

1. Plane or sand the top to a consistent thickness, then rip and crosscut it to size. It should fit into its rabbets leaving about a ⅛-in. gap at the sides and front, with the back edge flush to the case back.

2. Rout a ¼-in. by 8-in. cove in the rear edge of the top to serve as a pull (see "Ratchet Mechanism").

3. Rout a ¼-in. by ¼-in. by 17¼-in.-long groove into the top for the ledge (see **photo D** on p. 118). The groove should sit about 1 in. from the front edge of the top (see "Case Detail, Top View" on p. 118).

4. Make the ledge (see "Ledge Detail" on p. 119). Becker made his from maple, which contrasts nicely with the cherry. After dimensioning the ledge blank, saw or rout the

Photo B: Cutting the case sides and front from one board and reassembling the pieces in sequence creates a continuous, flowing grain pattern around the front of the desk.

RATCHET MECHANISM

The case top adjusts to various angles using a shopmade ratchet mechanism. Two pawls, which are connected to a hinge dowel and crossbar, engage in notches in two ratchet bars that are attached to the case bottom. Bullet catches in the top battens hold the pawl assembly up when not in use.

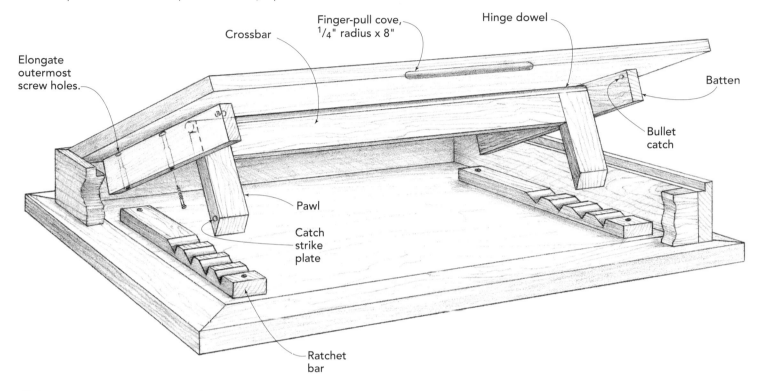

Crossbar

Finger-pull cove,
$^1/_4$" radius x 8"

Hinge dowel

Batten

Elongate
outermost
screw holes.

Bullet
catch

Pawl

Catch
strike
plate

Ratchet
bar

Photo C: Saw a rabbet in the top edges of the case sides and front to recess and support the case top.

tongue along the bottom edge. Then cut off
¾ in. of the tongue at each end with a small
handsaw. Use a file to round over the ends of
the tongue to match the ends of the groove in
the case top.

5. Round over the top edges of the ledge with
a block plane and round the ends with a chisel and file. Finish profiling the ends with
coarse sandpaper, then finish-sand with progressively finer grits.

6. Finish-sand the top before gluing the ledge
into its groove.

7. Lay out and drill five 14-mm-diameter
holes into the rear of the case front and into
the front edge of the top for the barrel hinges
(see **photo E**). Center the outermost holes
2¼-in. from the edges of the top (see "Case
Detail, Top View").

Photo D: A straight-
edge and a router
are used to cut the
groove for the ledge
in the case top.

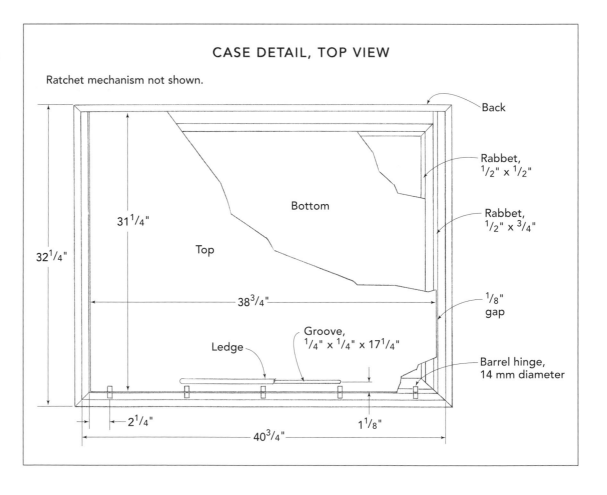

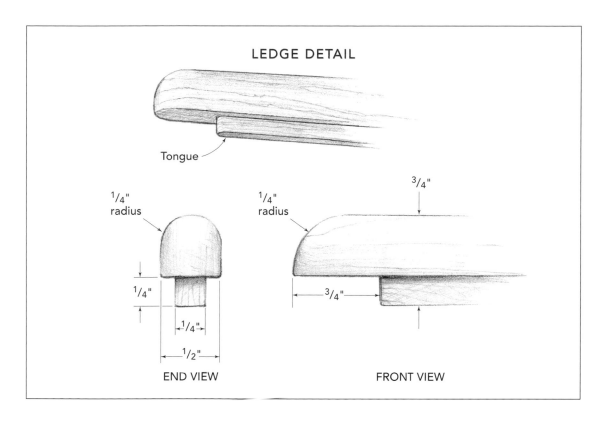

LEDGE DETAIL

Tongue

$\frac{1}{4}$"
radius

$\frac{1}{4}$"
radius

$\frac{3}{4}$"

$\frac{1}{4}$"

$\frac{1}{4}$"

$\frac{1}{2}$"

$\frac{3}{4}$"

END VIEW

FRONT VIEW

Photo E: Use a 14-mm-diameter bit to drill the holes for the barrel hinge mortises.

MAKING THE RATCHET MECHANISM

The ratchet mechanism consists of two wooden pawls that engage notches in two ratchet bars. The pawls, which are connected by a crossbar, are glued to a wooden dowel hinge that pivots in holes drilled through the top's battens. The ratchet bars are screwed to the case bottom (see "Ratchet Mechanism" on p. 117). Bullet catches installed in the battens hold the pawls to the top when not in use.

Making the pawl assembly

1. Dimension the hinge dowel, pawls, and crossbar. Becker joined the pawls to the crossbar with mortise-and-tenon joints (see "Pawl Assembly Detail" on p. 120). However, you could just as easily connect them with biscuits or dowels. Just be sure you adjust the length of the crossbar accordingly. Don't cut the miters on the ends of the pawls yet, or you may have difficulty clamping them to the hinge dowel.

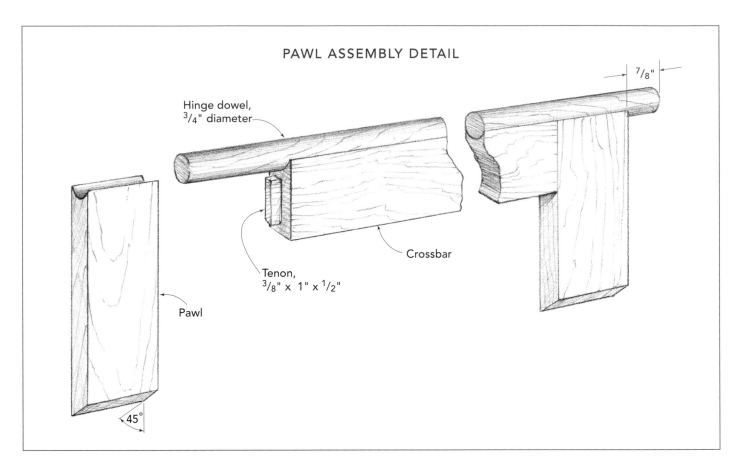

PAWL ASSEMBLY DETAIL

Hinge dowel,
$3/4$" diameter

$7/8$"

Tenon,
$3/8$" x 1" x $1/2$"

Crossbar

Pawl

45°

Photo F: Rout the cove in the pawl assembly using a ¾-in.-diameter corebox bit in a router table. The cove accommodates the wooden hinge dowel in the ratchet mechanism.

2. Cut the mortises in the pawls and the corresponding tenons on the ends of the crossbar. Then glue the three pieces together.

3. Plane or sand the pawl assembly flat, then rout a ¾-in.-diameter by ⅜-in.-deep cove along the entire length of the upper edge. This cove will accept the hinge dowel. The easiest and safest way to cut the cove is with a corebox bit mounted in a router table (see **photo F**).

4. Glue the pawl assembly to the hinge dowel, using as many clamps as necessary to get a tight fit. Make sure the assembly is centered on the dowel so there is about ⅞ in. left over on each end (see **photo G**).

5. Cut the miters on the ends of the pawls, then slightly round over the ends with sandpaper or a file.

Photo G: Glue the hinge dowel to the pawl assembly, leaving ⅞-in. overhang at each end to project through the holes in the case top battens.

Making the ratchet bars and battens

1. Dimension the stock for the ratchet bars.
2. Lay out the profile of the notches on the side of each bar (see "Case Detail, Side View" on p. 122).
3. Cut the notches with a stack dado cutter set up for a ¾-in.-wide cut. Tilt the stack dado 30 degrees on the table saw (see **photo H** on p. 122). For accuracy and efficiency, you can clamp the two ratchet bars together when making the cuts or you can make the notches on one wide piece, then rip it in half to form the two bars.
4. Sand the ratchet bars.
5. Cut the battens to size, then drill a ¾-in.-diameter hole through each for the hinge dowel (see "Case Detail, Side View" on p. 122).

Assembling the ratchet mechanism

1. Drill and counterbore three screw holes in each batten for fastening it to the case top. Elongate the outermost holes to allow the top to expand and contract with seasonal changes in humidity (see "Ratchet Mechanism" on p. 117).
2. Insert the ends of the hinge dowel into the holes in the battens and center the assembly on the underside of the top.
3. Screw the battens to the top, being careful not to exit the top. Don't use glue here, as it would prevent the top from moving and would make it difficult to remove the battens for possible repair or modification of the pawl assembly.

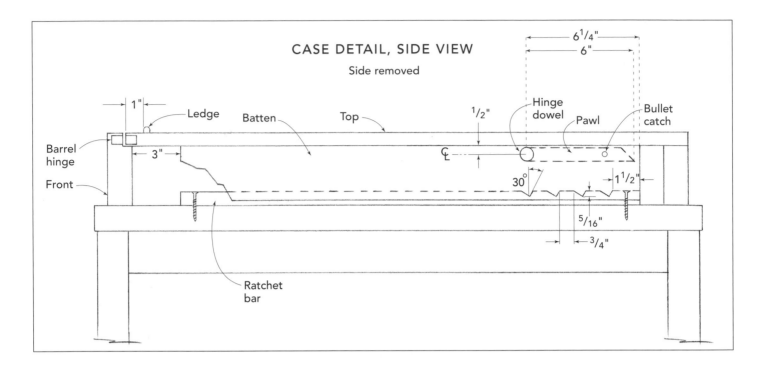

CASE DETAIL, SIDE VIEW

Side removed

6¼"

6"

1"

Ledge   Batten   Top   ½"   Hinge dowel   Pawl   Bullet catch

Barrel hinge

3"   C̶L̶

Front

30°   1½"

5/16"

¾"

Ratchet bar

Photo H: Cut the notches in the ratchet bars using a ¾-in.-wide stack dado tilted 30 degrees on the table saw.

4. Place the ratchet bars into the case and place the case top into its case wall rabbets. Tilt the top up enough to line up the ratchet bars to the pawls. Then remove the top and attach the ratchet bars to the case bottom with two countersunk screws each (see "Case Detail, Side View).

MAKING THE BRASS SCUFF PLATE

Becker cut the brass scuff plate on his bandsaw using a regular 6 tpi wood-cutting blade. As explained below, the trick to clean, accurate cutting is to sandwich the brass between a wooden template and a piece of backup scrap so the metal doesn't flex while being cut (see **photo I**). Sheet brass is available in various thicknesses from some hardware stores and metal-working shops.

1. Make a ¼-in.-thick plywood template from the scuff plate pattern (see "Scuff Plate Pattern" on p. 115).
2. Cut a sheet of brass slightly larger than the template.

Photo I: To cleanly bandsaw the brass scuff plate, you can keep it from flexing by sandwiching it between an upper plywood template and a backup scrap piece.

3. Cut a piece of ½-in.-thick scrap plywood an inch or so wider and longer than the template. This will be your cutting backup piece.
4. On the template, lay out a series of evenly spaced screw holes. The spacing should be attractive, and there should be enough holes to securely fasten the brass plate down. The thicker the brass, the fewer number of holes needed. If necessary, test the spacing on a piece of scrap brass.
5. Place the brass on a piece of scrap (not your backup piece) and set the template on top of it. Drill the holes using a bit that matches the outside thread diameter of a #3 flat-head screw.
6. After drilling the holes through the template and the brass, place the brass on your backup piece, with the template on top. Screw the brass and the template to your ½-in.-thick cutting backup piece.

7. Saw the brass to shape on the bandsaw, cutting as close to the edge of the template as possible (see **photo I**).
8. With the brass still sandwiched between the template and the backup scrap, sand the edges of the brass until they are flush with the template edges.
9. Remove the brass from the sandwich and countersink the holes to accommodate the heads of #3 flat-head brass screws. Be very careful not to drill too deep. You want the screw heads to lay dead flush with the brass.
10. Sand the scuff plate. Because the brass will be scraped and scuffed by shoes, it does not need a highly polished finish. Becker used 180-grit paper on a random orbit sander to give the brass a matte finish. Set the finished scuff plate aside for now.

FINISHING UP

All that's left is to attach the case to the base, apply a finish, hinge the top, and install the brass scuff plate.

1. Attach the case to the base by screwing up through the skirt into the case bottom. Becker used three 2½-in.-long drywall screws through each skirt, setting each one into a ½-in.-deep counterbore.
2. Give the entire desk a final light sanding and apply a finish. Because this desk was built for a professional office, Becker wanted a finish that could withstand a lot of wear and tear. He applied four coats of precatalyzed lacquer, sanding with progressively finer grits between each coat.
3. After the finish is dry, attach the top with the barrel hinges.
4. Install a bullet catch on each batten and its mating catch plate on the pawl (see "Ratchet Mechanism" on p. 117). The catches will hold the pawls up when not in use. If you prefer, you could install a sliding barrel bolt instead. It doesn't matter much what hardware you use, as long as it easily accessible from the front of the desk.
5. Finally, install the brass scuff plate on the top face of the front center stretcher using #3 flat-head brass screws.

Pedestal Desk

Paul and Michael Wilson, owners of Wilson Woodworking in Windsor, Vermont, have built a number of variations of the pedestal desk pictured here. The design can be easily modified to suit a variety of styles, shapes, and sizes. Sometimes the Wilsons replace one of the pedestals with a simple, standing panel. If the desk will hold a computer they often incorporate a keyboard tray instead of a center drawer. At times, they have even eliminated the feet by bringing the base all the way down to the floor. When building your own version, you can easily alter the size, number, and placement of the drawers to create a desk that suits your own needs (see "Design Options" on p. 130).

The desk draws on elements of Shaker design, yet the clean lines and bright, figured hard maple give it a modern look. The desk is constructed of a series of framed book-matched floating panels that are joined together to form the two pedestals.

Two pull-out boards, commercial drawer slides, and deep drawers make it practical and highly functional for a busy home or professional office. The pull-out boards above the top drawers expand the working area of the desk by more than 3 square ft. but slide out of the way when not in use. The entire assembly is strengthened and stiffened by the top, which is screwed to the pedestals. Although this desk is made of hard maple, cherry or walnut would be good choices as well.

Pedestal Desk

THIS DESK IS CONSTRUCTED OF A SERIES of frame-and-panel assemblies that incorporate the legs as frame members. Six of the eight legs are tapered at the foot and are complemented by the curved lower rails on the front and outermost case sides. The pull-out board runners do double-duty as cleats for attaching the top.

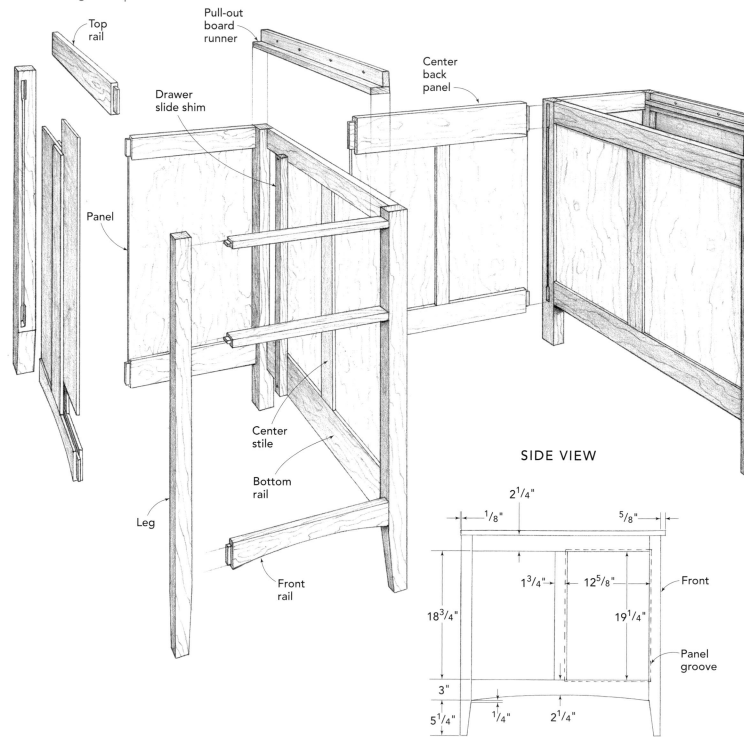

Top rail

Pull-out board runner

Drawer slide shim

Center back panel

Panel

Center stile

Bottom rail

Leg

Front rail

SIDE VIEW

$2^{1}/_{4}$"

$1/_{8}$"

$5/_{8}$"

$1^{3}/_{4}$"

$12^{5}/_{8}$"

Front

$18^{3}/_{4}$"

$19^{1}/_{4}$"

Panel groove

3"

$1/_{4}$"

$2^{1}/_{4}$"

$5^{1}/_{4}$"

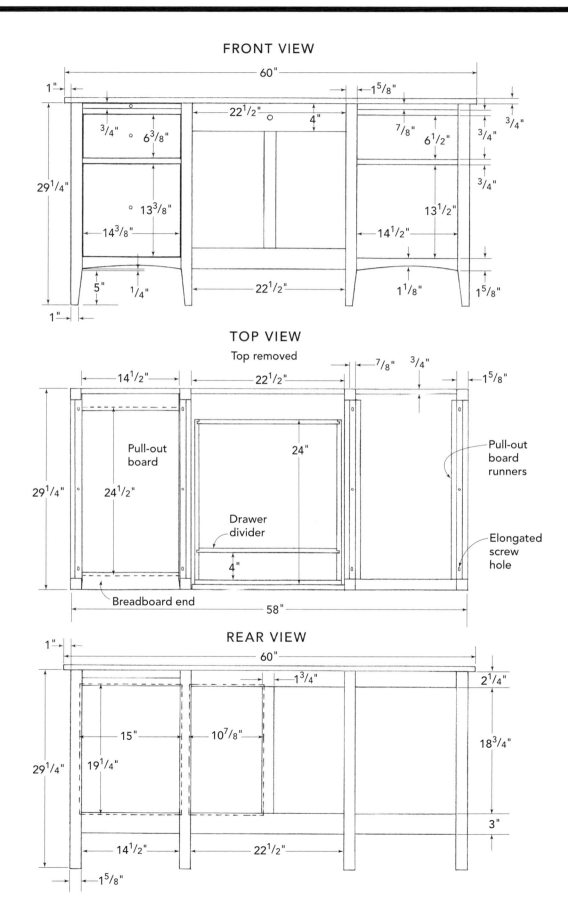

FRONT VIEW

TOP VIEW
Top removed

Pull-out board

24"

Drawer divider

Pull-out board runners

Elongated screw hole

Breadboard end

REAR VIEW

BUILDING THE DESK STEP-BY-STEP

CUT LIST FOR PEDESTAL DESK

1	Top	¾ in. x 30 in. x 60 in.
8	Legs	1⅝ in. x 1⅝ in. x 29¼ in.

Side Panels

4	Top rails	¾ in. x 2¼ in. x 27½ in. (including a ⅜-in. x 1¾-in. x ¾-in. tenon on both ends)
4	Bottom rails	¾ in. x 3 in. x 27½ in. (including a ⅜-in. x 2½-in. x ¾-in. tenon on both ends)
4	Center stiles	¾ in. x 1¾ in. x 19¼ in. (including a ⁵⁄₁₆-in. x 1¼-in. x ¼-in. tenon on both ends)
8	Panels	⁵⁄₁₆ in. x 12⅝ in. x 19¼ in.

Back Panels

2	Outer top rails	¾ in. x 2¼ in. x 16 in. (including a ⅜-in. x 1¾-in. x ¾-in. tenon on both ends)
1	Center top rail	¾ in. x 2¼ in. x 24 in. (including a ⅜-in. x 1¾-in. x ¾-in. tenon on both ends)
2	Outer bottom rails	¾ in. x 3 in. x 16 in. (including a ⅜-in. x 2½-in. x ¾-in. tenon on both ends)
1	Center bottom rail	¾ in. x 3 in. x 24 in. (including a ⅜-in. x 2½-in. x ¾-in. tenon on both ends)
1	Center stile	¾ in. x 1¾ in. x 19¼ in. (including a ⁵⁄₁₆-in. x 1¼-in. x ¼-in. tenon on both ends)
2	Outer panels	⁵⁄₁₆ in. x 15 in. x 19¼ in.
2	Center panels	⁵⁄₁₆ in. x 10⅞ in. x 19¼ in.

Front Rails

4	Upper rails	¾ in. x 1⅝ in. x 16 in. (including a ⅜-in. x 1⅛-in. x ¾-in. tenon on both ends)
2	Bottom rails	¾ in. x 1⅝ in. x 16 in. (including a ⅜-in. x 1⅛-in. x ¾-in. tenon on both ends)

NORMALLY I LIKE to start with the top when making a desk because it is usually the most visible part. With this desk, however, the floating side panels are the focal point, so I start with them, after which I glue up the top. Next, I make the legs, the frame-and-panel assemblies, and the front rails. Then I assemble the pedestals and connect them with the back center panel. Last, I make the drawers and pull-out boards, and attach the top.

MAKING THE FLOATING PANELS AND THE TOP

Each of the 12 floating panels is made from a wide board that is resawn and book-matched (see "Book-Matching" on p. 131). The desktop need not be book-matched, but should be laid out for a good grain match at the joints. Depending on the quality of your lumber, you will need a minimum of 25 to 30 board ft. of 4/4 material to make the floating panels and the top.

Making the panels and top

1. Select your best 4/4 stock for the panels. As you lay out the stock for each panel, carefully consider its position on the desk to achieve an overall visual balance.

2. Cut each panel blank to rough length and width, leaving each piece a few inches oversize in length and a bit wider than half the dimension of the finished panel.

3. Joint the long-grain edges of the stock, then draw a line across the edge of each piece for future reference when orienting the pieces for book-matching.

4. Resaw each panel blank in half on the bandsaw. Use a wide blade and a high fence. Set the angle of the fence to compensate for "drift" (see "Resawing" on p. 132).

CUT LIST FOR PEDESTAL DESK

Pull-Out Boards

2	Pull-out boards	¾ in. x 14¼ in. x 23⅝ in. (including a ⅜-in. x 14⅜-in. x ½-in. tenon on both ends)
1	Breadboard end	¾ in. x 2½ in. x 14⅜ in.
1	Breadboard end	¾ in. x 2½ in. x 14¼ in.
4	Runner side pieces	⅞ in. x ⅞ in. x 26 in.
4	Runner bottom pieces	¾ in. x 1⅝ in. x 26 in.

Top Left and Right Drawers

2	Drawer fronts	¾ in. x 6⅜ in. x 14⅜ in.
2	Box fronts	⅝ in. x 5½ in. x 13½ in.
4	Sides	⅝ in. x 5½ in. x 24 in.
2	Backs	⅝ in. x 4½ in. x 12⅞ in.
2	Bottoms	½ in. x 12⅞ in. x 23¹¹⁄₁₆ in.

Top Center Drawer

1	Drawer front	¾ in. x 4 in. x 22⅜ in.
1	Box front	⅝ in. x 3 in. x 21½ in.
2	Sides	⅝ in. x 3 in. x 24 in.
1	Back	⅝ in. x 2½ in. x 20⅞ in.
1	Drawer divider	⅝ in. x 2½ in. x 20⅞ in.
1	Bottom	¼ in. x 20⅞ in. x 23¹¹⁄₁₆ in.

Bottom Left and Right Drawers

2	Drawer fronts	¾ in. x 13⅜ in. x 14⅜ in.
2	Box fronts	⅝ in. x 12½ in. x 13½ in.
4	Sides	⅝ in. x 12½ in. x 24 in.
2	Backs	⅝ in. x 11½ in. x 12⅞ in.
2	Bottoms	½ in. x 12⅞ in. x 23¹¹⁄₁₆ in.

Hardware

5 pr.	Drawer slides	24 in. long

Design Options

STYLE CHANGES IN THE SIZE, position, and number of drawers greatly change the form of the base.

SINGLE-PEDESTAL DESK

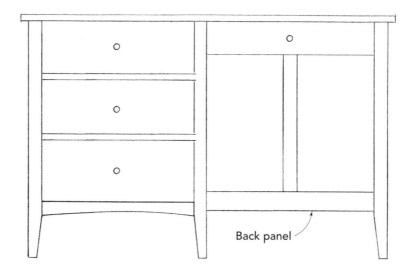

Back panel

DOUBLE-PEDESTAL DESK WITH BASE MOLDING

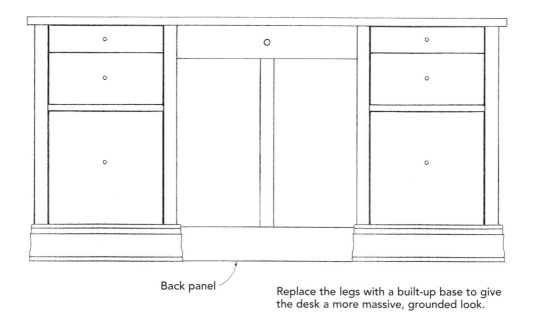

Back panel

Replace the legs with a built-up base to give the desk a more massive, grounded look.

BOOK-MATCHING

Book-matching is the practice of resawing a board into thinner pieces, then gluing the pieces edge to edge to create a mirrored effect with the grain.

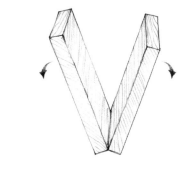

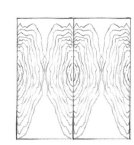

Board cut into two pieces and opened like a book

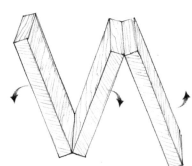

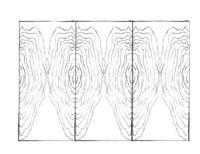

Board cut into multiple pieces

5. If the faces of the boards end up wavy or dished out in areas because of flawed resawing, surface them to a relatively uniform thickness.

6. Edge glue the halves of each panel together, being sure to align them so the grain pattern matches fairly well at the center. After removing the panels from the clamps, stack them on a flat bench with stickers between each one and a few heavy weights on top of the stack. This will minimize warpage as the panels wait to be fitted in their frames.

7. Lay out stock for the desktop, leaving the boards slightly oversize in length and width. Then surface them to approximate thickness and joint the edges.

8. Edge glue the boards to make the top.

MAKING THE LEGS

This desk has eight legs, six of which have a tapered "foot" at the bottom. The legs are connected by the frame-and-panel assemblies that make up the desk sides and back.

1. Lay out enough 8/4 stock to make the legs. Crosscut and rip the pieces slightly oversize.

2. Mill the pieces to $1\frac{5}{8}$ in. square. I joint two adjacent faces of each piece, then I run the pieces through a thickness planer to square up the remaining two faces.

3. Crosscut the legs to length, then mark the end of each to indicate the leg's position on the desk.

RESAWING ON THE BANDSAW

To make the book-matched panels for this desk, you'll need to resaw wide boards. The best way to do this is on a bandsaw equipped with the proper blade and a high fence.

Use the widest blade your bandsaw will handle. A wide blade won't flex as much as a narrow one and will cut easier and straighter. However, the width of blade you can use depends somewhat on your saw's power. For example, my saw will accommodate a ¾-in.-wide blade, but I find when using it that the motor bogs down during heavy cuts. So I generally use a ⅜-in.- or ½-in.-wide blade for resawing. I use a hooked-tooth blade with 3 tpi. The blade cuts aggressively and clears out the dust quickly. A blade with more teeth per inch will cut smoother but much more slowly.

When resawing relatively narrow boards, I often make the cut freehand. But when working with wide stock, I use a high fence as a guide. My fence is simply screwed together from scrap plywood. The important things are that it is sturdy; square to the table; and high enough to support a wide, heavy board.

Last, you will need to account for *blade drift*—the tendency of a bandsaw blade to pull to one side of the workpiece when cutting. The trick to cutting straight is to determine the angle of the drift, then set the fence to that angle. To do this, first gauge a line down the center of a piece of scrap that's about 18 in. long. Carefully cut to the line freehand to establish the angle of feed. When you're about halfway through, turn off the saw while keeping a firm grip on the workpiece to maintain its angle of feed. Trace the edge of the workpiece onto your saw table, then set your fence parallel to that line.

A high fence helps guide the workpiece when resawing wood on the bandsaw.

JOINERY DETAILS

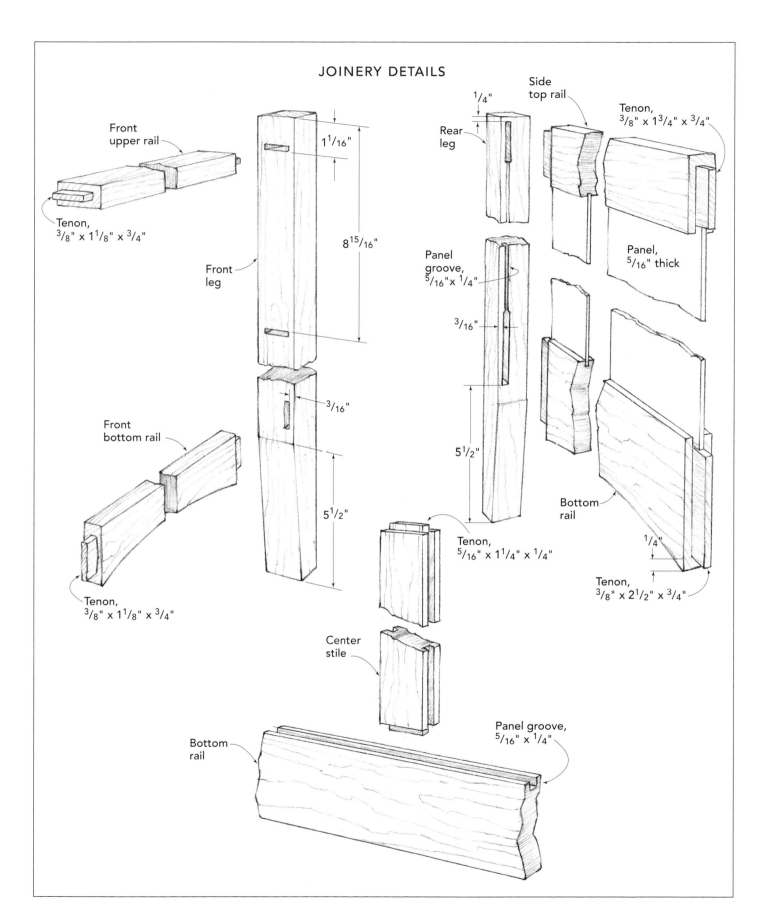

Front upper rail

Tenon,
$^3/_8$" x 1$^1/_8$" x $^3/_4$"

Front leg

1$^1/_{16}$"

8$^{15}/_{16}$"

$^3/_{16}$"

5$^1/_2$"

Front bottom rail

Tenon,
$^3/_8$" x 1$^1/_8$" x $^3/_4$"

Bottom rail

Center stile

$^1/_4$"

Side top rail

Rear leg

Tenon,
$^3/_8$" x 1$^3/_4$" x $^3/_4$"

Panel groove,
$^5/_{16}$" x $^1/_4$"

$^3/_{16}$"

5$^1/_2$"

Panel,
$^5/_{16}$" thick

Bottom rail

$^1/_4$"

Tenon,
$^3/_8$" x 2$^1/_2$" x $^3/_4$"

Tenon,
$^5/_{16}$" x 1$^1/_4$" x $^1/_4$"

Panel groove,
$^5/_{16}$" x $^1/_4$"

Photo B: A stiff pattern ensures that the taper on each leg will be uniform.

4. Lay out the mortises to accept the tenons on the rails (see "Joinery Details" on p. 133). Pay close attention to where and how each leg is positioned on the desk.

5. Cut the mortises. You can drill and chop them by hand, use a mortiser, or rout them using a plunge router guided by a router fence.

6. Rout the 5⁄16-in.-wide by 3⁄16-in.-deep panel grooves, centering them on the tenon mortises. I cut the grooves on a router table, but you could use a handheld router guided by a router fence.

7. Mark the tapers at the bottoms of the front legs and the outermost rear legs (see **photo B**). The two outermost front legs get a double taper, but the others are tapered on only one face (see "Pedestal Desk" on p. 126). The inner rear legs are not tapered.

8. Cut the tapers on a bandsaw, then smooth the cuts with a belt sander or handplane.

9. Sand only the mortised and grooved faces of the legs for right now, stopping just a bit short of the area where the ends of the rails will butt against the leg.

MAKING THE FRAME-AND-PANEL ASSEMBLIES

At this point, the only pieces needed to complete the pedestal assemblies are the stiles and rails that connect the sides, back, and front of the pedestals. They all get tenons on each end, so it makes sense to machine them all at once.

Cutting and fitting the rails and stiles

1. Mill stock for the rails and stiles. Rip and crosscut the pieces to size, being sure to include the length for the tenons on each end.

2. Cut the tenons, centering them on the ends of the stock (see "Joinery Details" on p. 133). I cut them on the table saw, using a dado head (see **photo C**).

3. Saw the ⁵⁄₁₆-in.-wide by ³⁄₁₆-in.-deep panel grooves, centering them across the edges of the stock. Although you could rout them, it's much quicker and cleaner to cut them on the table saw using a dado head.

4. Lay out the curves on the bottom front rails and the bottom rails of the outermost side panels (see "Pedestal Desk" on p. 126). To lay them out, run a pencil line against a thin strip of straight-grained stock that is held to the bottom corners of each rail and sprung upward the proper amount (see "Side View" on p. 126 and "Front View" on p. 127).

5. Use a bandsaw or jigsaw to cut the curves, and then sand the cut edges smooth (see **photo D**).

6. Sand the grooved edges of the rails, stopping a bit short of the areas where the center stiles meet the horizontal rails. Don't sand the faces of the rails yet.

Photo D: A spindle sander does a great job of smoothing curves.

Photo C: When cutting tenons on a table saw, use a stop block to prevent having to bury the dado head in an auxiliary fence.

Photo E: A table saw
crosscut sled allows
you to crosscut wide
panels squarely.

Fitting the panels

To fit the panels, you'll need to dry-clamp
each leg-rail-stile assembly in turn, then measure for each panel, and saw it to fit.

1. Dry-clamp each of the leg-rail-stile assemblies together to check the fit of the joinery
and to measure for the panels. Make sure the
assembly is square under clamp pressure, then
measure between the panel grooves to determine the sizes of the panels.

2. Mark out the length and width of each
panel. It should fit snugly between its top and
bottom grooves, but should be sized in width
to accommodate future expansion and contraction of the panel. If you're working during
the dry, winter season, allow more room. If it's
hot and humid, fit the panel more tightly.
(For more on frame-and-panel construction,
see "Dealing with Wood Movement" on
p. 13.) Lay out the width equally from the
center of the panel to ensure symmetry of the
book-match.

3. Trim each panel to size on the table saw
(see **photo E**).

4. After all of the panels have been fit, sand
them, and apply a couple coats of finish to
both sides of each one. If you wait to finish
them until after the desk is assembled, the
unfinished panel edges concealed in the
grooves could shrink away from the frame
later, exposing bare wood.

ASSEMBLING THE PEDESTALS

The best way to put the desk together is to
assemble the pedestal sides first, then attach
the pedestal backs and front rails between
the sides.

1. Glue up each of the four side assemblies,
being careful to keep glue out of the panel
grooves. Make sure that each assembly is flat
and square under clamp pressure.

2. After the glue is dry, sand the faces of the assemblies to level and smooth the joints. Take care not to scratch the panels. Don't sand the outer edges of the legs yet.

3. After the side assemblies are dry, glue the back and the front rails between the sides. Again, avoid getting glue on the back panels. Make sure the pedestals are square under clamp pressure. Otherwise, they may sit unevenly, making the drawers difficult to fit.

4. Sand the rails flush to the legs, avoiding the edge of the inner rear legs where the center back panel will be attached.

5. Glue the center frame-and-panel assembly between the pedestals, then square up the entire base and hold it square by screwing lengths of scrap wood across the top and bottom of the pedestals near the front. This will also allow you to move the desk around the shop if necessary.

6. After the glue is dry, sand the center panel joints flat and smooth.

MAKING THE DRAWERS

The drawer boxes are constructed with dovetails in the front and rabbet-and-dado joints in the back. The drawers will ride on commercially made drawer slides that require ½ in. clearance on each side of the drawer (see **photo F**). The solid maple drawer fronts are screwed to the drawer boxes and conceal the slides that are attached to the sides of the box.

1. Mill and cut the drawer parts to size. Make the drawer fronts from solid maple. You can use a secondary wood for the drawer box; the Wilsons used pine. The side drawers have ½-in.-thick plywood bottoms, but the bottom of the shallow center drawer is made from ¼-in.-thick plywood.

2. Lay out the dovetails, remembering that the drawer bottom groove should pass through a tail, not a pin (see "Drawer

Photo F: The drawers are installed with commercially made, side-mounted drawer slides.

Drawer Construction

THE DRAWERS ARE CONSTRUCTED with through dovetails at the front and a rabbet-and-dado joint at the back. Lay out the dovetail spacing to your liking, making sure that the bottom groove passes through a tail, not a pin. The bottom of the top center drawer is ¼" thick. All of the other bottoms are ½" thick.

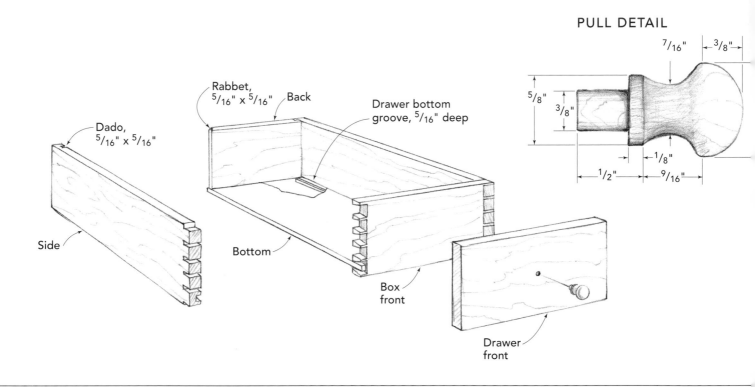

PULL DETAIL

Dado, $^5/_{16}$" x $^5/_{16}$"

Side

Rabbet, $^5/_{16}$" x $^5/_{16}$"   Back

Bottom

Drawer bottom groove, $^5/_{16}$" deep

Box front

Drawer front

Construction"). You can use any spacing you like, but keep the dovetail angle somewhere between 12 and 14 degrees.

3. Cut the dovetails.

4. Using a dado head in a table saw, cut the rabbet-and-dado joints for the rear of the boxes and the pencil divider joint in the center drawer (see "Top View" on p. 127).

5. Cut the grooves for the bottoms, aligning them just under the bottom edge of the drawer back.

6. Glue the boxes together, then slide the bottoms into their grooves. Make sure the drawers are square, then attach the bottoms to the drawer backs with a few screws.

7. After the glue has dried, sand the drawer boxes so the joints are all flush and the sharp

edges are slightly eased. You should also sand the drawer fronts now.

8. Screw the drawer slides to the drawer boxes and to the insides of the cabinet, following the manufacturer's instructions. You can attach the front of the slides to the inside face of the front legs, but you'll need to shim out the slides at their centers and rear ends to bring them flush to the front end. The easiest approach is to screw a long piece of ⅞-in.- thick stock to the case rails at the midpoint and rear of the drawer slides. (see "Pedestal Desk" on p. 126).

9. After installing the drawer boxes, attach the fronts. The Wilsons apply a couple of dabs of hot-melt glue to the drawer front, then stick it on the box, quickly aligning it for a

DRAWER FRONT ADJUSTERS

Properly attaching drawer fronts to their drawer boxes can be a fight. Even if you manage to get a consistent gap between a drawer front and its opening, things can still change. Drawer front adjusters are a slick solution. They are basically thick plastic washers with a movable threaded insert at the center that allows for slight shifting of a drawer front.

To install the adjusters, begin by drilling two 20-mm-diameter by $\frac{7}{6}$-in.-deep holes in the backside of the drawer front. Then place 20-mm-diameter dowel centers in the holes. Position the drawer front in its opening and press it firmly against the drawer box to transfer the hole centers to the front of the drawer box. Next, drill holes at those loca-

tions to accept the machine screws that thread into the adjusters. Replace each dowel center with a drawer adjuster, pounding it in with a hammer.

Attach the drawer fronts by inserting machine screws through the box front into the drawer adjusters. Snug up the screws, but not too tightly, then position the front exactly where you want it; the metal inserts in the drawer adjusters allow for as much as $\frac{3}{16}$ in. movement in any direction. When you're happy, tighten the screws. On large drawers, I reinforce the attachment with a screw in each corner of the drawer front.

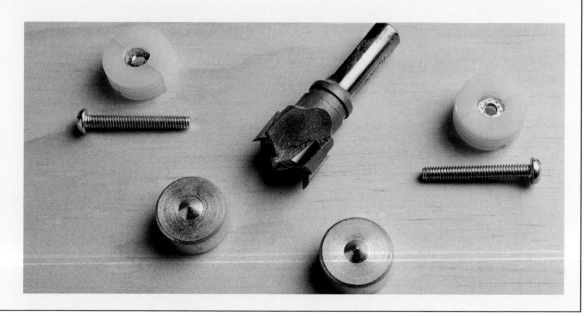

Drawer adjusters, a 20-mm bit, dowel centers, and machine screws.

consistent gap between the drawer front and its opening. Then they anchor the front in place with several screws. You could also use double-sided tape or short nails to align the front before anchoring it with screws. Personally, I prefer to use drawer front adjusters (see "Drawer Front Adjusters").

10. Drill the holes for the pulls, then turn the pulls, but don't install them yet. It is easier to finish the drawer fronts with them off. (Instead of making your own pulls, you can buy them from many mail-order woodworking supply companies.)

MAKING THE PULL-OUT BOARDS

The breadboard ends on the pull-out boards help keep the boards flat. Dowels that ride in slotted holes in the tongue allow the boards to expand and contract with seasonal changes. The front breadboard end is a bit wider than the main body of the board to maintain a close gap in its opening, while allowing the board to expand and contract (see **photo G**).

Building the pull-out boards

1. Glue up the main body of the pull-out boards. To minimize potential warpage, use several narrow pieces rather than one or two wide ones, and edge join the pieces so that the annular rings are reversed on adjacent pieces (see "Breadboard End Construction").

2. Plane or sand the blanks to a thickness of slightly more than ¾ in., but don't bother finish-sanding them at this point. Do try to maintain a consistent thickness on each board, because the thickness of the tongue—thus the breadboard end joint—will be affected by it.

3. Cut the breadboard ends to width and length. Notice that the front piece is ⅛ in. longer than the back.

4. Cut the groove in the edge of each breadboard end. You could rout them, but it's much quicker to cut them on the table saw (see **photo H**).

Photo G: The front edge of the pull-out board is feathered back with a sander to maintain a tight fit at the front while allowing for cross-grain expansion and contraction of the board inside the case.

BREADBOARD END CONSTRUCTION

Breadboard end construction is a great way to keep a panel flat. Because the grain of the breadboard ends is perpendicular to the grain of the board, the ends prevent movement of the board. Elongated holes in the tongue allow the board to expand and contract naturally with the seasons.

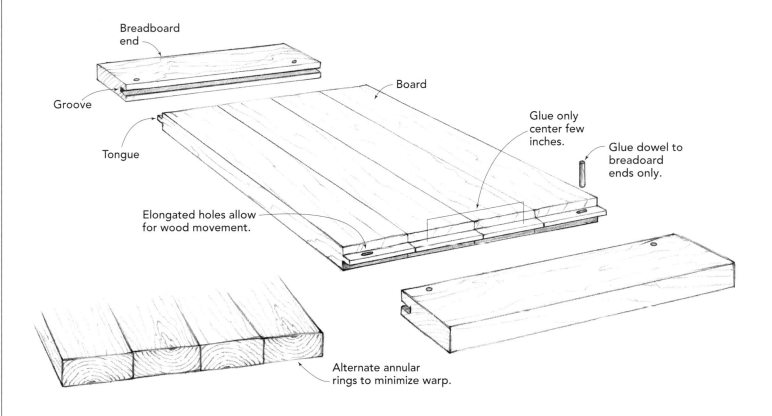

Breadboard end

Groove

Tongue

Board

Glue only center few inches.

Glue dowel to breadoard ends only.

Elongated holes allow for wood movement.

Alternate annular rings to minimize warp.

Photo H: Saw the grooves in the breadboard ends using a dado head setup for a cut slightly narrower than the thickness of the tongue on the pull-out board. Make the first pass, then flip the board end for end and make another pass. This will center the groove in the workpiece.

Photo I: The tongue on each end of the pull-out board should fit snugly into the groove on the breadboard end, but not so tightly that you have to pound it in with a hammer.

5. Cut the opposing rabbets that create the tongue on each end of the board. I saw the rabbets on the table saw, using a dado head. Aim for a snug fit (see **photo I**).

6. With the breadboard ends in place, drill two ¼-in.-diameter holes completely through each breadboard end and tongue, 1 in. or so in from the edge of the tongue.

7. Remove the breadboard ends, and lengthen the drill holes a bit with a round file (see **photo J**). Be careful not to widen the holes toward the end of the tongue, or the breadboard end may pull away in use.

8. Attach the breadboard ends by applying just a bit of glue on the center few inches of the tongue and a small drop of glue on the very end of each peg.

9. Sand both faces of the pull-out boards so they are smooth. Sand the ends of the rear breadboard ends so they're flush with the edges of the main body.

10. Belt sand the rear section of the front breadboard end to feather it back to the body of the board (see **photo G** on p. 140).

Installing the pull-out boards

The boards ride on two-piece, L-shaped runners that are attached to the sides of the pedestals. The runners also serve as screw cleats for attaching the desktop (see "Pedestal Desk" on p. 126).

1. Make each runner by gluing and screwing together its side and bottom pieces.

2. Sand the inside faces of the runners so the pull-out boards will slide freely.

Photo J: Elongated holes in the pull-out board tongue allow the board to expand and contract around the pegs without splitting.

3. Drill screw holes through the runners for attaching the top. Elongate the outermost holes about ¼ in. with a round file to allow the top to expand and contract over time.

4. Glue and screw the runners to the pedestal side top rails.

5. Insert each pull-out board into its opening. When fully inserted, the front edge of the pull-out board should be flush to the front rails. Trim or shim at the rear if necessary.

FINISHING UP

1. Place the top on the desk and attach it with screws through the pull-out board runners.

2. Give the entire desk a final finish-sanding.

3. Apply a finish. Paul Wilson sprayed on two coats of a precatalyzed lacquer for the tough finish necessary in a commercial office environment. However, you may simply want to wipe a couple of coats of oil onto the base. The top should get additional protection, though—two or three coats of polyurethane or water-based lacquer would do the trick. It's also wise to finish the underside of the top to help prevent the wood from absorbing moisture unevenly and cupping or cracking.

SOURCES

General project supplies and hardware, including drawer slides, knobs and pulls, hinges, dowels, and finishing supplies, are available from the following companies.

CUSTOM SERVICE HARDWARE
1170 Wauwatosa Rd.
Cedarburg, WI 53012
(800) 882-0009

LEE VALLEY TOOLS
P.O. Box 1780
Ogdensburg, NY 13669-6780
(800) 871-8158

ROCKLER WOODWORKING AND HARDWARE
4365 Willow Dr.
Medina, MN 55340-9701
(800) 279-4441

VAN DYKE'S RESTORERS
P.O. Box 278
Woonsocket, SD 57385
(800) 558-1234

WOODCRAFT
560 Airport Industrial Park
P.O. Box 1686
Parkersburg, WV 26102-1686
(800) 225-1153

WOODWORKER'S SUPPLY
1108 N. Glenn Rd.
Casper, WY 82601-1698
(800) 853-9663

Veneers and veneering supplies are available from the following companies.

CERTAINLY WOOD
13000 Route 78
East Aurora, NY 14052-9508
(716) 655-0206

CONSTANTINE'S
2050 Eastchester Rd.
Bronx, NY 10461
(800) 223-8087

BIBLIOGRAPHY

Aronson, Joseph. *The Encyclopedia of Furniture*. Crown Publishing.

Boger, Louise Ade. *The Complete Guide to Furniture Styles*. Waveland Press.

Chippendale, Thomas. *The Gentleman & Cabinetmaker's Director*. Dover Publications.

Duncan, Alastair. *Art Deco Furniture: The French Designers*. Thames and Hudson Ltd.

Garth, Graves. *The Woodworker's Guide to Furniture Design*. Popular Woodworking Books.

Hepplewhite and Co. *The Cabinet-Maker and Upholsterer's Guide*. Dover Publications.

Morley, John. *The History of Furniture: Three Thousand Years of Style, Form and Design*. Bulfinch Press.

Pye, David. *The Nature and Aesthetics of Design*. Van Nostrand Reinhold Co.

Pye, David. *The Nature and Aesthetics of Workmanship*. Cambridge University Press.

Sheraton, Thomas. *The Cabinet-Maker and Upholsterer's Drawing Book*. Dover Publications.

Thonet Co. *Thonet Bentwood & Other Furniture*. Dover Publications.

PROJECT DESIGNERS

Lap Desk
Andy Charron
28 River St.
P.O. Box 552
Windsor, VT 05089

Fall-Front Desk and **Book Stand**
Terry Moore
11 Summer St.
Newport, NH 03773

Pedestal Desk
Michael and Paul Wilson
Wilson Woodworking
28 River St.
Windsor, VT 05089

Greene and Greene Writing Desk
Thomas Stangeland
800 Mercer St.
Seattle, WA 98109

Stand-Up Desk
Jim Becker
45 A Street
P.O. Box 802
Wilder, VT 05088

Laptop Desk
Stephen Lauziere
13 Old Kings Hwy.
Lebanon, NH 03766

METRIC CONVERSION CHART

INCHES	CENTIMETERS	MILLIMETERS	INCHES	CENTIMETERS	MILLIMETERS
⅛	0.3	3	13	33.0	330
¼	0.6	6	14	35.6	356
⅜	1.0	10	15	38.1	381
½	1.3	13	16	40.6	406
⅝	1.6	16	17	43.2	432
¾	1.9	19	18	45.7	457
⅞	2.2	22	19	48.3	483
1	2.5	25	20	50.8	508
1¼	3.2	32	21	53.3	533
1½	3.8	38	22	55.9	559
1¾	4.4	44	23	58.4	584
2	5.1	51	24	61.0	610
2½	6.4	64	25	63.5	635
3	7.6	76	26	66.0	660
3½	8.9	89	27	68.6	686
4	10.2	102	28	71.1	711
4½	11.4	114	29	73.7	737
5	12.7	127	30	76.2	762
6	15.2	152	31	78.7	787
7	17.8	178	32	81.3	813
8	20.3	203	33	83.8	838
9	22.9	229	34	86.4	864
10	25.4	254	35	88.9	889
11	27.9	279	36	91.4	914
12½	30.5	305			

INDEX

INDEX

Q
Queen Anne-style fall-front desk, 5

R
Rabbet joints, 13, *13*
    drawer corner technique, *18*
Rails in Stand-up desk, 112, 113, *113*
Ratchet mechanism in Stand-up desk, 116, *117*, 118, *118*, 119, *119*, 120, *120*, 121, *121*, 122
Recesses for drawer pull, 66, *67*, 69, *69*
Resawing on a bandsaw, 129, 131, *131*, *132*

S
Scuff plate, *110*, 114, *115*, 122–23, *123*
Secret drawers/compartments, 13, *14*
Shaker design elements:
    in Lap desk, 21
    in Pedestal desk, 125
Shelves, 6, *6*, 7, *7*, 8, *9*, 10, *10*
    fixed, in Fall-front desk, 105–106, *106*
Skirts for Laptop desk, 62–63
Slide-out tray in Laptop desk, 55, *56*, *58–59*, 65–66, *66*
Sliding dovetail drawer corner technique, *19*
Splines in Greene and Greene writing desk, 79, *79*, 80, *80*
Square pegs in Greene and Greene writing desk, 87, *87*
Stand-up desk:
    barrel hinges in top, 118, *119*
    base joinery, 112, 113, *113*
    brass scuff plate, 122–23, *123*
    bullet catches, *117*, 119, 123
    constructing case box, 115–16, *116*, *117*, 118, *118*
    ledge detail, 116, 118, *118*
    mortise-and-tenon joinery, 114, *114*, 115
    rails in base, 112, 113, *113*

ratchet mechanism detail, 116, *117*, 118, *118*, 119, *119*, 120, *120*, 121, *121*, 122
    stretchers in base, 112, 113, *113*
    views of, *108*, *110*, *111*, *112*
Stangeland, Thomas, 71
Stickly, Gustav, 71
Stiles in Laptop desk, 63–64, *64*
Storage needs, 8, *9*, 10, *10*
Stretchers:
    for Book stand base, 38–39, 40, *40*
    in Fall-front desk, 96–97, *97*
    in Stand-up desk, 112, 113, *113*
String inlays in Book stand, 42, 45, *45*, *46*, 49, *49*

T
Tapering jigs, 25

V
Veneering:
    applying, 49, *49*
    assembly of pieces, 47, *47*, 48, *48*, 49, *49*
    drawer case, 40, 42, *42*, 43, 44, *44*, 45, *45*

W
Warping, prevention of, 68, *68*
Wedged through tenon, *97*
Wood materials, 10, *10*, 11, *11*, 71
Wood movement, preventing, 13, 16, *16*, 17, 68, *68*
Work surface, sizes of, 7, *7*
Writing surfaces, 4–5